TERENCE RATTIGAN

Born in 1911, a scholar at Harrow and at Trinity College, Oxford, Terence Rattigan had his first long-running hit in the West End at the age of twenty-five: *French Without Tears* (1936). His next play, *After the Dance* (1939), opened to euphoric reviews yet closed under the gathering clouds of war, but with *Flare Path* (1942) Rattigan embarked on an almost unbroken series of successes, with most plays running in the West End for at least a year and several making the transition to Broadway: *While the Sun Shines* (1943), *Love in Idleness* (1944), *The Winslow Boy* (1946), *The Browning Version* (performed in double-bill with *Harlequinade*, 1948), *Who is Sylvia?* (1950), *The Deep Blue Sea* (1952), *The Sleeping Prince* (1953) and *Separate Tables* (1954). From the mid-fifties, with the advent of the 'Angry Young Men', he enjoyed less success on stage, though *Ross* (1960) and *In Praise of Love* (1973) were well received. As well as seeing many of his plays turned into successful films, Rattigan wrote a number of original plays for television from the fifties onwards. He was knighted in 1971 and died in 1977.

**Other titles by the same author
published by Nick Hern Books**

After the Dance

The Browning Version and *Harlequinade*

Cause Célèbre

The Deep Blue Sea

First Episode

Flare Path

French Without Tears

In Praise of Love

Love in Idleness

Rattigan's Nijinsky
(adapted from Rattigan's screenplay by Nicholas Wright)

Separate Tables

Who is Sylvia? and *Duologue*

The Winslow Boy

Terence Rattigan

ROSS

Introduced by
Dan Rebellato

NICK HERN BOOKS
London
www.nickhernbooks.co.uk

A Nick Hern Book

This edition of *Ross* first published in Great Britain in 2016 as a paperback original by Nick Hern Books Limited, The Glasshouse, 49a Goldhawk Road, London W12 8QP. *Ross* was first published in 1960 by Hamish Hamilton Limited

Copyright © 1960 Trustees of the Terence Rattigan Trust
Introduction copyright © 2016 Dan Rebellato

Cover image: © Chronicle / Alamy Stock Photo; Image concept: SWD for Chichester Festival Theatre

Designed and typeset by Nick Hern Books, London
Printed in the UK by Mimeo Ltd, Huntingdon, Cambridgeshire PE29 6XX

A CIP catalogue record for this book is available from the British Library

ISBN 978 1 84842 578 1

Woodland CARBON
www.woodlandcarbon.co.uk
NICK HERN BOOKS
Printed on Carbon Captured paper

Terence Rattigan (1911–1977)

Terence Rattigan stood on the steps of the Royal Court Theatre, on 8 May 1956, after the opening night of John Osborne's *Look Back in Anger*. Asked by a reporter what he thought of the play, he replied, with an uncharacteristic lack of discretion, that it should have been retitled 'Look how unlike Terence Rattigan I'm being.'[1] And he was right. The great shifts in British theatre, marked by Osborne's famous premiere, ushered in kinds of playwriting which were specifically unlike Rattigan's work. The pre-eminence of playwriting as a formal craft, the subtle tracing of the emotional lives of the middle classes – those techniques which Rattigan so perfected – fell dramatically out of favour, creating a veil of prejudice through which his work even now struggles to be seen.

Terence Mervyn Rattigan was born on 10 June 1911, a wet Saturday a few days before George V's coronation. His father, Frank, was in the diplomatic corps and Terry's parents were often posted abroad, leaving him to be raised by his paternal grandmother. Frank Rattigan was a geographically and emotionally distant man, who pursued a string of little-disguised affairs throughout his marriage. Rattigan would later draw on these memories when he created Mark St Neots, the bourgeois Casanova of *Who is Sylvia?* Rattigan was much closer to his mother, Vera Rattigan, and they remained close friends until her death in 1971.

Rattigan's parents were not great theatregoers, but Frank Rattigan's brother had married a Gaiety Girl, causing a minor family uproar, and an apocryphal story suggests that the 'indulgent aunt' reported as taking the young Rattigan to the theatre may have been this scandalous relation.[2] And when, in the summer of 1922, his family went to stay in the country cottage of the drama critic Hubert Griffiths, Rattigan avidly worked through his extensive library of playscripts. Terry went to Harrow in 1925, and there maintained both his somewhat illicit theatregoing habit and his insatiable reading, reputedly devouring every play in the school library. Apart from contemporary authors like Galsworthy, Shaw and Barrie, he also read the plays of Chekhov, a writer whose crucial influence he often acknowledged.[3]

His early attempts at writing, while giving little sign of his later sophistication, do indicate his ability to absorb and reproduce his own theatrical experiences. There was a ten-minute melodrama about the Borgias entitled *The Parchment*, on the cover of which the author recommends with admirable conviction that a suitable cast for this work might comprise 'Godfrey Tearle, Gladys Cooper, Marie Tempest, Matheson Lang, Isobel Elsom, Henry Ainley... [and] Noël Coward'.[4] At Harrow, when one of his teachers demanded a French playlet for a composition exercise, Rattigan, undaunted by his linguistic shortcomings, produced a full-throated tragedy of deception, passion and revenge which included the immortal curtain line: 'COMTESSE. (*Souffrant terriblement*.) Non! non! non! Ah non! Mon Dieu, non!'[5] His teacher's now famous response was 'French execrable: theatre sense first class'.[6] A year later, aged fifteen, he wrote *The Pure in Heart,* a rather more substantial play showing a family being pulled apart by a son's crime and the father's desire to maintain his reputation. Rattigan's ambitions were plainly indicated on the title pages, each of which announced the author to be 'the famous playwrite and author T. M. Rattigan.'[7]

Frank Rattigan was less than keen on having a 'playwrite' for a son and was greatly relieved when in 1930, paving the way for a life as a diplomat, Rattigan gained a scholarship to read History at Trinity, Oxford. But Rattigan's interests were entirely elsewhere. A burgeoning political conscience that had led him to oppose the compulsory Officer Training Corps parades at Harrow saw him voice pacifist and socialist arguments at college, even supporting the controversial Oxford Union motion 'This House will in no circumstances fight for its King and Country' in February 1933. The rise of Hitler (which he briefly saw close at hand when he spent some weeks in the Black Forest in July 1933) and the outbreak of the Spanish Civil War saw his radical leanings deepen and intensify. Rattigan never lost his political compassion. After the war he drifted towards the Liberal Party, but he always insisted that he had never voted

Conservative, despite the later conception of him as a Tory playwright of the establishment.[8]

Away from the troubled atmosphere of his family, Rattigan began to gain in confidence as the contours of his ambitions and his identity moved more sharply into focus. He soon took advantage of the university's theatrical facilities and traditions. He joined the Oxford Union Dramatic Society (OUDS), where contemporaries included Giles Playfair, George Devine, Peter Glenville, Angus Wilson and Frith Banbury. Each year, OUDS ran a one-act play competition and in Autumn 1931 Rattigan submitted one. Unusually, it seems that this was a highly experimental effort, somewhat like Konstantin's piece in *The Seagull*. George Devine, the OUDS president, apparently told the young author, 'Some of it is absolutely smashing, but it goes too far.'[9] Rattigan was instead to make his first mark as a somewhat scornful reviewer for the student newspaper, *Cherwell*, and as a performer in the Smokers (OUDS's private revue club), where he adopted the persona and dress of 'Lady Diana Coutigan', a drag performance which allowed him to discuss leading members of the Society with a barbed camp wit.[10]

That the name of his Smokers persona echoed the contemporary phrase, 'queer as a coot', indicates Rattigan's new-found confidence in his homosexuality. In February 1932, Rattigan played a tiny part in the OUDS production of *Romeo and Juliet*, which was directed by John Gielgud and starred Peggy Ashcroft and Edith Evans (women undergraduates were not admitted to OUDS, and professional actresses were often recruited). Rattigan's failure to deliver his one line correctly raised an increasingly embarrassing laugh every night (an episode which he reuses to great effect in *Harlequinade*). However, out of this production came a friendship with Gielgud and his partner, John Perry. Through them, Rattigan was introduced to theatrical and homosexual circles, where his youthful 'school captain' looks were much admired.

A growing confidence in his sexuality and in his writing led to his first major play. In 1931, he shared rooms with a contemporary of his, Philip Heimann, who was having an affair with Irina Basilevich, a mature student. Rattigan's own feelings for Heimann completed an eternal triangle that formed the basis

of the play he co-wrote with Heimann, *First Episode*. This play
was accepted for production in Surrey's 'Q' theatre; it was
respectfully received and subsequently transferred to the
Comedy Theatre in London's West End, though carefully shorn
of its homosexual subplot. Despite receiving only £50 from this
production (and having put £200 into it), Rattigan immediately
dropped out of college to become a full-time writer.

Frank Rattigan was displeased by this move, but made a deal
with his son. He would give him an allowance of £200 a year
for two years and let him live at home to write; if at the end of
that period, he had had no discernible success, he would enter
a more secure and respectable profession. With this looming
deadline, Rattigan wrote quickly. *Black Forest*, an O'Neill-
inspired play based on his experiences in Germany in 1933,
is one of the three that have survived. Rather unwillingly, he
collaborated with Hector Bolitho on an adaptation of the latter's
novel, *Grey Farm*, which received a disastrous New York
production in 1940. Another project was an adaptation of *A Tale
of Two Cities*, written with Gielgud; this fell through at the last
minute when Donald Albery, the play's potential producer,
received a complaint from actor-manager John Martin-Harvey
who was beginning a farewell tour of his own adaptation, *The
Only Way*, which he had been performing for forty-five years.
As minor compensation, Albery invited Rattigan to send him
any other new scripts. Rattigan sent him a play provisionally
titled *Gone Away*, based on his experiences in a French-
language summer school in 1931. Albery took out a nine-month
option on it, but no production appeared.

By mid-1936, Rattigan was despairing. His father had secured
him a job with Warner Brothers as an in-house screenwriter,
which was reasonably paid; but Rattigan wanted success in the
theatre, and his desk-bound life at Teddington Studios seemed
unlikely to advance this ambition. By chance, one of Albery's
productions was unexpectedly losing money, and the wisest
course of action seemed to be to pull the show and replace it
with something cheap. Since *Gone Away* required a relatively
small cast and only one set, Albery quickly arranged for a
production. Harold French, the play's director, had only one
qualm: the title. Rattigan suggested *French Without Tears*,
which was immediately adopted.

After an appalling dress rehearsal, no one anticipated the rapturous response of the first-night audience, led by Cicely Courtneidge's infectious laugh. The following morning Kay Hammond, the show's female lead, discovered Rattigan surrounded by the next day's reviews. 'But I don't believe it,' he said. 'Even *The Times* likes it.'[11]

French Without Tears played over 1000 performances in its three-year run and Rattigan was soon earning £100 a week. He moved out of his father's home, wriggled out of his Warner Brothers contract, and dedicated himself to spending the money as soon as it came in. Partly this was an attempt to defer the moment when he had to follow up this enormous success. In the event, both of his next plays were undermined by the outbreak of war.

After the Dance, an altogether more bleak indictment of the Bright Young Things' failure to engage with the iniquities and miseries of contemporary life, opened, in June 1939, to euphoric reviews; but only a month later the European crisis was darkening the national mood and audiences began to dwindle. The play was pulled in August after only sixty performances. *Follow My Leader* was a satirical farce closely based on the rise of Hitler, co-written with an Oxford contemporary, Tony Goldschmidt (writing as Anthony Maurice in case anyone thought he was German). It suffered an alternative fate. Banned from production in 1938, owing to the Foreign Office's belief that 'the production of this play at this time would not be in the best interests of the country',[12] it finally received its premiere in 1940, by which time Rattigan and Goldschmidt's mild satire failed to capture the real fears that the war was unleashing in the country.

Rattigan's insecurity about writing now deepened. An interest in Freud, dating back to his Harrow days, encouraged him to visit a psychiatrist that he had known while at Oxford, Dr Keith Newman. Newman exerted a Svengali-like influence on Rattigan and persuaded the pacifist playwright to join the RAF as a means of curing his writer's block. Oddly, this unorthodox treatment seemed to have some effect; by 1941, Rattigan was writing again. On one dramatic sea crossing, an engine failed, and with everyone forced to jettison all excess baggage and possessions, Rattigan threw the hard covers and blank pages from the notebook containing his new play, stuffing the precious manuscript into his jacket.

Rattigan drew on his RAF experiences to write a new play, *Flare Path*. Bronson Albery and Bill Linnit who had supported *French Without Tears* both turned the play down, believing that the last thing that the public wanted was a play about the war.[13] H. M. Tennent Ltd., led by the elegant Hugh 'Binkie' Beaumont, was the third management offered the script; and in 1942, *Flare Path* opened in London, eventually playing almost 700 performances. Meticulously interweaving the stories of three couples against the backdrop of wartime uncertainty, Rattigan found himself a box-office success. Beaumont, already on the way to becoming the most powerful and successful West End producer of the era, was an influential ally for Rattigan. There is a curious side-story to this production; Dr Keith Newman decided to watch 250 performances of this play and write up the insights that his 'serial attendance' had afforded him. George Bernard Shaw remarked that such playgoing behaviour 'would have driven me mad; and I am not sure that [Newman] came out of it without a slight derangement'. Shaw's caution was wise.[14] In late 1945, Newman went insane and eventually died in a psychiatric hospital.

Meanwhile, Rattigan had achieved two more successes; the witty farce, *While the Sun Shines*, and the more serious, though politically clumsy, *Love in Idleness* (retitled *O Mistress Mine* in America). He had also co-written a number of successful films, including *The Day Will Dawn, Uncensored, The Way to the Stars* and an adaptation of *French Without Tears*. By the end of 1944, Rattigan had three plays running in the West End, a record only beaten by Somerset Maugham's four in 1908.

Love in Idleness was dedicated to Henry 'Chips' Channon, the Tory MP who had become Rattigan's lover. Channon's otherwise gossipy diaries record their meeting very discreetly: 'I dined with Juliet Duff in her little flat... also there, Sibyl Colefax and Master Terence Rattigan, and we sparkled over the Burgundy. I like Rattigan enormously, and feel a new friendship has begun. He has a flat in Albany.'[15] Tom Driberg's rather less discreet account fleshes out the story: Channon's 'seduction of the playwright was almost like the wooing of Danaë by Zeus –

every day the playwright found, delivered to his door, a splendid present – a case of champagne, a huge pot of caviar, a Cartier cigarette box in two kinds of gold... In the end, of course, he gave in, saying apologetically to his friends, "How can one *not*?".'[16] It was a very different set in which Rattigan now moved, one that was wealthy and conservative, the very people he had criticised in *After the Dance*. Rattigan did not share the complacency of many of his friends, and his next play revealed a deepening complexity and ambition.

For a long time, Rattigan had nurtured a desire to become respected as a serious writer; the commercial success of *French Without Tears* had, however, sustained the public image of Rattigan as a wealthy, young, light-comedy writer-about-town.[17] With *The Winslow Boy*, which premiered in 1946, Rattigan began to turn this image around. In doing so he entered a new phase as a playwright. As one contemporary critic observed, this play 'put him at once into the class of the serious and distinguished writer'.[18] The play, based on the Archer-Shee case in which a family attempted to sue the Admiralty for a false accusation of theft against their son, featured some of Rattigan's most elegantly crafted and subtle characterisation yet. The famous second curtain, when the barrister Robert Morton subjects Ronnie Winslow to a vicious interrogation before announcing that 'The boy is plainly innocent. I accept the brief', brought a joyous standing ovation on the first night. No less impressive is the subtle handling of the concept of 'justice' and 'rights' through the play of ironies which pits Morton's liberal complacency against Catherine Winslow's feminist convictions.

Two years later, Rattigan's *Playbill*, comprising the one-act plays *The Browning Version* and *Harlequinade*, showed an ever deepening talent. The latter is a witty satire of the kind of touring theatre encouraged by the new Committee for the Encouragement of Music and Arts (CEMA, the immediate forerunner of the Arts Council). But the former's depiction of a failed, repressed Classics teacher evinced an ability to choreograph emotional subtleties on stage that outstripped anything Rattigan had yet demonstrated.

Adventure Story, which in 1949 followed hard on the heels of *Playbill*, was less successful. An attempt to dramatise the emotional dilemmas of Alexander the Great, Rattigan seemed unable to escape the vernacular of his own circle, and the epic scheme of the play sat oddly with Alexander's more prosaic concerns.

Rattigan's response to both the critical bludgeoning of this play and the distinctly lukewarm reception of *Playbill* on Broadway was to write a somewhat extravagant article for the *New Statesman*. 'Concerning the Play of Ideas' was a desire to defend the place of 'character' against those who would insist on the pre-eminence in drama of ideas.[19] The essay is not clear and is couched in such teasing terms that it is at first difficult to see why it should have secured such a fervent response. James Bridie, Benn Levy, Peter Ustinov, Sean O'Casey, Ted Willis, Christopher Fry and finally George Bernard Shaw all weighed in to support or condemn the article. Finally Rattigan replied in slightly more moderate terms to these criticisms insisting (and the first essay reasonably supports this) that he was not calling for the end of ideas in the theatre, but rather for their inflection through character and situation.[20] However, the damage was done (as, two years later, with his 'Aunt Edna', it would again be done). Rattigan was increasingly being seen as the arch-proponent of commercial vacuity.[21]

The play Rattigan had running at the time added weight to his opponents' charge. Originally planned as a dark comedy, *Who is Sylvia?* became a rather more frivolous thing both in the writing and the playing. Rattled by the failure of *Adventure Story*, and superstitiously aware that the new play was opening at the Criterion, where fourteen years before *French Without Tears* had been so successful, Rattigan and everyone involved in the production had steered it towards light farce and obliterated the residual seriousness of the original conceit.

Rattigan had ended his affair with Henry Channon and taken up with Kenneth Morgan, a young actor who had appeared in *Follow My Leader* and the film of *French Without Tears*. However, the relationship had not lasted and Morgan had for a while been seeing someone else. Rattigan's distress was compounded one day in February 1949, when he received a message that Morgan had killed himself. Although horrified, Rattigan soon began to conceive an idea for a play. Initially it was to have concerned a homosexual relationship, but Beaumont, his producer, persuaded him to change the relationship to a heterosexual one.[22] At a time when the Lord Chamberlain refused to allow any plays to be staged that featured homosexuality, such a proposition would have been a commercial impossibility. The result is one of the finest examples of Rattigan's craft. The story of Hester Collyer, trapped in a relationship with a man incapable of returning her love, and her transition from attempted suicide to groping, uncertain self-determination is handled with extraordinary economy, precision and power. The depths of despair and desire that Rattigan plumbs have made *The Deep Blue Sea* one of his most popular and moving pieces.

1953 saw Rattigan's romantic comedy *The Sleeping Prince*, planned as a modest, if belated, contribution to the Coronation festivities. However, the project was hypertrophied by the insistent presence of Laurence Olivier and Vivien Leigh in the cast and the critics were disturbed to see such whimsy from the author of *The Deep Blue Sea*.

Two weeks after its opening, the first two volumes of Rattigan's *Collected Plays* were published. The preface to the second volume introduced one of Rattigan's best-known, and most notorious creations: Aunt Edna. 'Let us invent,' he writes, 'a character, a nice respectable, middle-class, middle-aged, maiden lady, with time on her hands and the money to help her pass it.'[23] Rattigan paints a picture of this eternal theatregoer, whose bewildered disdain for modernism ('Picasso – "those dreadful reds, my dear, and why three noses?"')[24] make up part of the particular challenge of dramatic writing. The intertwined commercial and cultural pressures that the audience brings with it exert considerable force on the playwright's work.

Rattigan's creation brought considerable scorn upon his head. But Rattigan is neither patronising nor genuflecting towards Aunt Edna. The whole essay is aimed at demonstrating the crucial role of the audience in the theatrical experience. Rattigan's own sense of theatre was *learned* as a member of the audience, and he refuses to distance himself from this woman: 'despite my already self-acknowledged creative ambitions I did not in the least feel myself a being apart. If my neighbours gasped with fear for the heroine when she was confronted with a fate worse than death, I gasped with them'.[25] But equally, he sees his job as a writer to engage in a gentle tug-of-war with the audience's expectations: 'although Aunt Edna must never be made mock of, or bored, or befuddled, she must equally not be wooed, or pandered to or cosseted'.[26] The complicated relation between satisfying and surprising this figure may seem contradictory, but as Rattigan notes, 'Aunt Edna herself is indeed a highly contradictory character.'[27]

But Rattigan's argument, as in the 'Play of Ideas' debate before it, was taken to imply an insipid pandering to the unchallenging expectations of his audience. Aunt Edna dogged his career from that moment on and she became such a byword for what theatre should *not* be that in 1960, the Questors Theatre, Ealing, could title a triple-bill of Absurdist plays, 'Not For Aunt Edna'.[28]

Rattigan's next play did help to restore his reputation as a serious dramatist. *Separate Tables* was another double-bill, set in a small Bournemouth hotel. The first play develops Rattigan's familiar themes of sexual longing and humiliation while the second pits a man found guilty of interfering with women in a local cinema against the self-appointed moral jurors in the hotel. The evening was highly acclaimed and the subsequent Broadway production a rare American success.

However, Rattigan's reign as the leading British playwright was about to be brought to an abrupt end. In a car from Stratford to London, early in 1956, Rattigan spent two and a half hours informing his Oxford contemporary George Devine why the new play he had discovered would not work in the theatre. When Devine persisted, Rattigan answered 'Then I know nothing about plays.' To which Devine replied, 'You know everything about plays, but you don't know a fucking thing about *Look Back in Anger*.'[29] Rattigan only barely attended the first night. He and Hugh Beaumont wanted to leave at the interval until the critic T. C. Worsley persuaded them to stay.[30]

The support for the English Stage Company's initiative was soon overwhelming. Osborne's play was acclaimed by the influential critics Kenneth Tynan and Harold Hobson, and the production was revived frequently at the Court, soon standing as the banner under which that disparate band of men (and women), the Angry Young Men, would assemble. Like many of his contemporaries, Rattigan decried the new movements, Beckett and Ionesco's turn from Naturalism, the wild invective of Osborne, the passionate socialism of Wesker, the increasing influence of Brecht. His opposition to them was perhaps intemperate, but he knew what was at stake: 'I may be prejudiced, but I'm pretty sure it won't survive,' he said in 1960, 'I'm prejudiced because if it *does* survive, I know I won't.'[31]

Such was the power and influence of the new movement that Rattigan almost immediately seemed old-fashioned. And from now on, his plays began to receive an almost automatic panning. His first play since *Separate Tables* (1954) was *Variation on a Theme* (1958). But between those dates the critical mood had changed. To make matters worse, there was the widely publicised story that nineteen-year-old Shelagh Delaney had written the successful *A Taste of Honey* in two weeks after having seen *Variation on a Theme* and deciding that she could do better. A more sinister aspect of the response was the increasingly open accusation that Rattigan was dishonestly concealing a covert homosexual play within an apparently heterosexual one. The two champions of Osborne's play, Tynan and Hobson, were joined by Gerard Fay in the *Manchester Guardian* and Alan Brien in the *Spectator* to ask 'Are Things What They Seem?'[32]

When he is not being attacked for smuggling furtively homosexual themes into apparently straight plays, Rattigan is also criticised for lacking the courage to 'come clean' about his sexuality, both in his life and in his writing.[33] But neither of these criticisms really hit the mark. On the one hand, it is rather disingenuous to suggest that Rattigan should have 'come out'. The 1950s were a difficult time for homosexual men. The flight to the Soviet Union of Burgess and Maclean in 1951 sparked off a major witch-hunt against homosexuals, especially those in prominent positions. Cecil Beaton and Benjamin Britten were rumoured to be targets.[34] The police greatly stepped up the investigation and entrapment of homosexuals and prosecutions rose dramatically at the end of the forties, reaching a peak in 1953–4. One of their most infamous arrests for importuning, in October 1953, was that of John Gielgud.[35]

But neither is it quite correct to imply that somehow Rattigan's plays are *really* homosexual. This would be to misunderstand the way that homosexuality figured in the forties and early fifties. Wartime London saw a considerable expansion in the number of pubs and bars where homosexual men (and women) could meet. This network sustained a highly sophisticated system of gestural and dress codes, words and phrases that could be used to indicate one's sexual desires, many of them drawn from theatrical slang. But the illegality of any homosexual activity ensured that these codes could never become *too* explicit, *too* clear. Homosexuality, then, was explored and experienced through a series of semi-hidden, semi-open codes of behaviour; the image of the iceberg, with the greater part of its bulk submerged beneath the surface, was frequently employed.[36] And this image is, of course, one of the metaphors often used to describe Rattigan's own playwriting.

Reaction came in the form of a widespread paranoia about the apparent increase in homosexuality. The fifties saw a major drive to seek out, understand, and often 'cure' homosexuality. The impetus of these investigations was to bring the unspeakable and underground activities of, famously, 'Evil Men' into the open, to make it fully visible. The Wolfenden Report of 1957 was, without doubt, a certain kind of liberalising document in its recommendation that consensual sex between adult men in private be legalised. However the other side of its effect is to reinstate the integrity of those boundaries – private/public, hidden/exposed, homosexual/heterosexual – which homosexuality was broaching. The criticisms of Rattigan are precisely part of this same desire to divide, clarify and expose.

Many of Rattigan's plays were originally written with explicit homosexual characters (*French Without Tears*, *The Deep Blue Sea* and *Separate Tables*, for example), which he then changed.[37] But many more of them hint at homosexual experiences and activities: the relationship between Tony and David in *First Episode*, the Major in *Follow My Leader* who is blackmailed over an incident in Baghdad ('After all,' he explains, 'a chap's only human, and it was a deuced hot night – '),[38] the suspiciously polymorphous servicemen of *While the Sun Shines*, Alexander the Great and T. E. Lawrence from

Adventure Story and *Ross*, Mr Miller in *The Deep Blue Sea* and several others. Furthermore, rumours of Rattigan's own bachelor life circulated fairly widely. As indicated above, Rattigan always placed great trust in the audiences of his plays, and it was the audience that had to decode and reinterpret these plays. His plays cannot be judged by the criterion of 'honesty' and 'explicitness' that obsessed a generation after Osborne. They are plays which negotiate sexual desire through structures of hint, implications and metaphor. As David Rudkin has suggested, 'the craftsmanship of which we hear so much loose talk seems to me to arise from deep psychological necessity, a drive to organise the energy that arises out of his own pain. Not to batten it down but to invest it with some expressive clarity that speaks immediately to people, yet keeps itself hidden.'[39]

The shifts in the dominant view of both homosexuality and the theatre that took place in the fifties account for the brutal decline of Rattigan's career. He continued writing, and while *Ross* (1960) was reasonably well received, his ill-judged musical adaptation of *French Without Tears*, *Joie de Vivre* (1960), was a complete disaster, not assisted by a liberal bout of laryngitis among the cast, and the unexpected insanity of the pianist.[40] It ran for four performances.

During the sixties, Rattigan was himself dogged with ill-health: pneumonia and hepatitis were followed by leukaemia. When his death conspicuously failed to transpire, this last diagnosis was admitted to be incorrect. Despite this, he continued to write, producing the successful television play *Heart to Heart* in 1962, and the stage play *Man and Boy* the following year, which received the same sniping that greeted *Variation on a Theme*. In 1964, he wrote *Nelson – a Portrait in Miniature* for Associated Television, as part of a short season of his plays.

It was at this point that Rattigan decided to leave Britain and live abroad. Partly this decision was taken for reasons of health; but partly Rattigan just seemed no longer to be welcome. Ironically, it was the same charge being levelled at Rattigan that he had faced in the thirties, when the newspapers thundered against the those who had supported the Oxford Union's pacifist motion as 'woolly-minded Communists, practical jokers and sexual indeterminates'.[41] As he confessed in an interview late in his life, 'Overnight almost, we were told we were old-fashioned and effete and corrupt and finished, and... I somehow accepted Tynan's verdict and went off to Hollywood to write film scripts.'[42] In 1967 he moved to Bermuda as a tax exile. A stage adaptation of his Nelson play, as *Bequest to the Nation*, had a lukewarm reception.

Rattigan had a bad sixties, but his seventies seemed to indicate a turnaround in his fortunes and reputation. At the end of 1970, a successful production of *The Winslow Boy* was the first of ten years of acclaimed revivals. In 1972, Hampstead Theatre revived *While the Sun Shines*, and a year later the Young Vic was praised for its *French Without Tears*. In 1976 and 1977 *The Browning Version* was revived at the King's Head and *Separate Tables* at the Apollo. Rattigan briefly returned to Britain in 1971, pulled partly by his renewed fortune and partly by the fact that he was given a knighthood in the New Year's honours list. Another double-bill followed in 1973: *In Praise of Love* comprised the weak *Before Dawn* and the moving tale of emotional concealment and creativity, *After Lydia*. Critical reception was more respectful than usual, although the throwaway farce of the first play detracted from the quality of the second.

Cause Célèbre, commissioned by BBC Radio and others, concerned the Rattenbury case, in which Alma Rattenbury's aged husband was beaten to death by her eighteen-year-old lover. Shortly after its radio premiere, Rattigan was diagnosed with bone cancer. Rattigan's response, having been through the false leukaemia scare in the early sixties, was to greet the news with unruffled elegance, welcoming the opportunity to 'work harder and indulge myself more'.[43] The hard work included a play about the Asquith family and a stage adaptation of *Cause Célèbre*, but, as production difficulties began to arise over the latter, the Asquith play slipped out of Rattigan's grasp. Although very ill, he returned to Britain, and on 4 July 1977, he was taken by limousine from his hospital bed to Her Majesty's Theatre, where he watched his last ever premiere. A fortnight later he had a car drive him around the West End where two of his plays were then running before boarding the plane for the last time. On 30 November 1977, in Bermuda, he died.

As Michael Billington's perceptive obituary noted, 'his whole work is a sustained assault on English middle-class values: fear of emotional commitment, terror in the face of passion, apprehension about sex'.[44] In death, Rattigan began once again to be seen as someone critically opposed to the values with which he had so long been associated, a writer dramatising dark moments of bleak compassion and aching desire.

Notes

1. Quoted in Rattigan's *Daily Telegraph* obituary (1 December 1977).

2. Michael Darlow and Gillian Hodson. *Terence Rattigan: The Man and His Work*. London and New York: Quartet Books, 1979, p. 26.

3. See, for example, Sheridan Morley. 'Terence Rattigan at 65.' *The Times*. (9 May 1977).

4. Terence Rattigan. Preface. *The Collected Plays of Terence Rattigan: Volume Two*. London: Hamish Hamilton, 1953, p. xv.

5. *Ibid.,* p. viii.

6. *Ibid.,* p. vii.

7. *Ibid.,* p. vii.

8. cf. Sheridan Morley, *op. cit.*

9. Humphrey Carpenter. *OUDS: A Centenary History of the Oxford University Dramatic Society*. With a Prologue by Robert Robinson. Oxford: Oxford University Press, 1985, p. 123.

10. Rattigan may well have reprised this later in life. John Osborne, in his autobiography, recalls a friend showing him a picture of Rattigan performing in an RAF drag show: 'He showed me a photograph of himself with Rattigan, dressed in a *tutu*, carrying a wand, accompanied by a line of aircraftsmen, during which Terry had sung his own show-stopper, 'I'm just about the oldest fairy in the business. I'm quite the oldest fairy that you've ever seen''.' John Osborne. *A Better Class of Person: An Autobiography, Volume I 1929–1956*. London: Faber and Faber, 1981, p. 223.

11. Darlow and Hodson *op. cit.*, p. 83.

12. Norman Gwatkin. Letter to Gilbert Miller, 28 July 1938. in: *Follow My Leader*. Lord Chamberlain's Correspondence: LR 1938. [British Library].

13. Richard Huggett. *Binkie Beaumont: Eminence Grise of the West Theatre 1933–1973*. London: Hodder & Stoughton, 1989, p. 308.

14. George Bernard Shaw, in: Keith Newman. *Two Hundred and Fifty Times I Saw a Play: or, Authors, Actors and Audiences*. With the facsimile of a comment by Bernard Shaw. Oxford: Pelagos Press, 1944, p. 2.

15. Henry Channon. *Chips: The Diaries of Sir Henry Channon*. Edited by Robert Rhodes James. Harmondsworth: Penguin, 1974, p. 480. Entry for 29 September 1944.

16. Tom Driberg. *Ruling Passions*. London: Jonathan Cape, 1977, p. 186.

17. See, for example, Norman Hart. 'Introducing Terence Rattigan,' *Theatre World*. xxxi, 171. (April 1939). p. 180 or Ruth Jordan. 'Another Adventure Story,' *Woman's Journal*. (August 1949), pp. 31–32.

18. Audrey Williamson. *Theatre of Two Decades*. New York and London: Macmillan, 1951, p. 100.

19. Terence Rattigan. 'Concerning the Play of Ideas,' *New Statesman and Nation*. (4 March 1950), pp. 241–242.

20 Terence Rattigan. 'The Play of Ideas,' *New Statesman and Nation*. (13 May 1950), pp. 545–546. See also Susan Rusinko, 'Rattigan versus Shaw: The 'Drama of Ideas' Debate'. in: *Shaw: The Annual of Bernard Shaw Studies: Volume Two*. Edited by Stanley Weintraub. University Park, Penn: Pennsylvania State University Press, 1982. pp. 171–78.

21. John Elsom writes that Rattigan's plays 'represented establishment writing'. *Post-War British Drama*. Revised Edition. London: Routledge, 1979, p. 33.

22. B. A. Young. *The Rattigan Version: Sir Terence Rattigan and the Theatre of Character*. Hamish Hamilton: London, 1986, pp. 102–103; and Darlow and Hodson, *op. cit.*, p. 196, 204n.

23. Terence Rattigan. *Coll. Plays: Vol. Two. op. cit.*, pp. xi–xii.

24. *Ibid.*, p. xii.

25. *Ibid.*, p. xiv.

26. *Ibid.*, p. xvi.

27. *Ibid.*, p. xviii.

28. Opened on 17 September 1960. cf. *Plays and Players*. vii, 11 (November 1960).

29. Quoted in Irving Wardle. *The Theatres of George Devine*. London: Jonathan Cape, 1978, p. 180.

30. John Osborne. *Almost a Gentleman: An Autobiography, Volume II 1955–1966*. London: Faber and Faber, 1991, p. 20.

31. Robert Muller. 'Soul-Searching with Terence Rattigan.' *Daily Mail*. (30 April 1960).

32. The headline of Hobson's review in the *Sunday Times*, 11 May 1958.

33. See, for example, Nicholas de Jongh. *Not in Front of the Audience: Homosexuality on Stage*. London: Routledge, 1992, pp. 55–58.

34. Kathleen Tynan. *The Life of Kenneth Tynan*. Corrected Edition. London: Methuen, 1988, p. 118.

35. Cf. Jeffrey Weeks. *Coming Out: Homosexual Politics in Britain from the Nineteenth Century to the Present*. Revised and Updated Edition. London and New York: Quartet, 1990, p. 58; Peter Wildeblood. *Against the Law*. London: Weidenfeld and Nicolson, 1955, p. 46. The story of Gielgud's arrest may be found in Huggett, *op. cit.,* pp. 429–431. It was Gielgud's arrest which apparently inspired Rattigan to write the second part of *Separate Tables*, although again, thanks this time to the Lord Chamberlain, Rattigan had to change the Major's offence to a heterosexual one. See Darlow and Hodson, *op. cit.*, p. 228.

36. See, for example, Rodney Garland's novel about homosexual life in London, *The Heart in Exile*. London: W. H. Allen, 1953, p. 104.

37. See note 36; and also 'Rattigan Talks to John Simon,' *Theatre Arts*. 46 (April 1962), p. 24.

38. Terence Rattigan and Anthony Maurice. *Follow My Leader*. Typescript. Lord Chamberlain Play Collection: 1940/2. Box 2506. [British Library].

39. Quoted in Darlow and Hodson, *op. cit.,* p. 15.

40. B. A. Young, *op. cit.,* p. 162.
41. Quoted in Darlow and Hodson, *op. cit.,* p. 56.
42. Quoted in Sheridan Morley, *op. cit.*
43. Darlow and Hodson, *op. cit.,* p. 308.
44. *Guardian.* (2 December 1977).

Ross

Ross is, without question, the most atypical play in Rattigan's canon of work. To someone familiar with his intense domestic dramas like *The Deep Blue Sea* or *Separate Tables*, it will be startling to read a play set in the desert, with terrorists and guerrillas blowing up train lines, and Arab Nationalists debating British foreign policy. Late in the play, the play's anti-hero, T. E. Lawrence, delivers a speech which would not be out of place in one of the 'In Yer Face' plays of the 1990s: 'Just outside the village we saw a child with a bayonet wound in his neck – but he was still alive. […] That was only the first thing we saw. Then we went into the village […and saw] the bodies of eighteen women, all bayoneted obscenely, two of them pregnant' (p.110).

And yet *Ross* was Terence Rattigan's second most commercially successful play (after the light comedy *When the Sun Shines*), playing for nearly two years at the Theatre Royal Haymarket, one of London's biggest theatres. When it closed in March 1962, it had been seen by over two-thirds of a million people. This is despite it being, as one reviewer acknowledged at the time, 'by far, his most ambitious play to date'.[1] It was particularly important to Rattigan. He admitted before the play opened, 'I have always wanted to be something better than just a Shaftesbury Avenue boy. My credo is that the audience is the judge, but my aim has always been to write a masterpiece'.[2]

Unfortunately, *Ross* coincided with the sharp downturn in Rattigan's reputation. Although it received some of the best and most respectful reviews of his career, the goodwill it had earned him was snuffed out two months later by *Joie de Vivre*, a disastrous musical adaptation of *French Without Tears* that was booed at the opening and closed within a week. It took twenty-five years for his reputation to recover and *Ross*'s reappraisal has been slow coming.

In some ways, Rattigan's shifting reputation reflects that of his protagonist, T. E. Lawrence. Rattigan's first great success came only a year after Lawrence died, his reputation and mystique at its height. Both men's standing suffered in the 1960s, and it has only been in recent years that a more balanced appraisal has once again allowed their merits to be seen.

The pairing of Rattigan and Lawrence may seem odd to contemporary eyes. One of them an adventurer and horseman, terrorist and saboteur; the other an urbane and witty West End playwright. The differences are very marked though it's striking that none of the first reviewers thought anything odd about Terry wanting to write about T. E. In fact, an examination of Lawrence's life and achievement, as well as the posthumous debates that surrounded his reputation, will reveal the reasons for Rattigan's keen interest in Lawrence of Arabia.

T. E. Lawrence

'Lawrence' was born in Carnarvon on August 1888. The name is in inverted commas because he and his siblings were the product of a then-scandalous liaison between the master of a house and his governess, and the surname was an invention – the first of many under which Lawrence lived his life. Researching a dissertation at Oxford on crusader castles in the Middle East, Lawrence developed a deep fascination for the Arab people and when the First World War broke out, he took the opportunity to sign up and help the Arab nationalist forces in their determination to topple the ruling Ottoman Empire. It is Lawrence's role in the Arab Revolt that is the basis of his fame and the source of his greatest controversies. It will be important to explain the background of the revolt to understand in outline the significance of what he is thought by some to have achieved.

As war approached, Germany made the strategic decision to form an alliance with the Ottomans, who ruled an empire out of Turkey that stretched from Bosnia in the North to Yemen in the South, and reached as far along the southern Mediterranean as Algeria.[3] The alliance was valuable to Germany because it created an effective barrier between Britain and France on one side and their entente ally Russia on the other. In the event of a war, this would disrupt the movement of troops, supplies and munitions and slow down communications. In addition,

Germany believed that the Ottoman Sultan's sway over the largely Muslim territories of North Africa would give him the power to call for *jihad* against the British and French, diverting their attention and resources and expediting a European victory. Initially, things went the German and Ottoman way. A British attack on Gallipoli in 1915, aiming to liberate the Dardanelles and open up an access route between East and West through the Black Sea, was defeated by the Ottomans, as was an assault on Mesopotamia the following year.[4]

However, the Ottomans' control of the Arab world was not so secure. In 1908, the co-called 'Young Turks' rose up against the Sultan's autocratic rule and forced him to restore the constitution and parliamentary democracy, which had been suspended over a quarter of a century earlier. Initially, this was popular in the Arab world, but enthusiasm waned when it became clear that few other reforms were forthcoming and that the Young Turks in fact wanted to see greater centralisation of power – with a concomitant reduction of regional autonomy. On the eve of war, Sharif Husayn,[5] the Arab ruler of Mecca, had been defying Turkish administrative encroachment on his province. Believing, understandably, that his resistance would soon lead to his dismissal, he secretly sent his son Abdullah to Cairo to open talks with British officials, hoping for their support, as they had supported the ruler of Kuwait when he too came into conflict with the Ottoman rulers in 1899. When Husayn intercepted intelligence that his overthrow was imminent, he also made discreet overtures, via his other son Feisal, to Arab nationalist groups.

These developments converged in March 1916 with a pledge from the British High Commissioner in Egypt, Sir Henry McMahon, that if Husayn would lead the Arabs in revolt against the Turks, Britain would support the cause of Arab Independence. At the beginning of January the first shots were fired in an Arab Revolt against Turkey. Husayn and his Arabist forces made some early gains, but by the late summer the Turks were fighting back.

Into this near-stalemate came Captain T. E. Lawrence, welcomed for his local knowledge, though not, at first, for his military strategy. After visiting Feisal, he concluded that the mixture of foreign and indigenous troops was not working and recommended, to Britain's relief, that money and equipment should be supplied to Feisal's Arab forces to continue the job themselves, with some limited British tactical support. Now adopting exclusively Arab dress, Lawrence led assaults against Turkish forces along the Red Sea, encouraging Feisal and Abdullah to coordinate strategy, and pinning the Ottomans back to Medina. He took part in several desert raids and was centrally involved in blowing up sections of the Hejaz Railway that was a core part of Turkish communications between Medina in the South and Damascus in the North.

During one of these expeditions in Deraa he was caught, taken for a deserter and brought before the bey, the name for a district governor. By Lawrence's own account, he repelled the bey's sexual advances, for which he was tortured and sexually assaulted. Left for dead, he managed to escape. (The episode will play a significant role in *Ross*.) He rejoined the battle and, having already been instrumental in the capture of Akaba (with Bedouin leader Auda Abu Tayi), he helped to take Tafileh and Damascus.

However, Lawrence's enthusiasm for the war was fading fast. The promises made by McMahon earlier in the war were not to be kept. In fact, the British had made several contradictory agreements about the post-war partition of Ottoman Arab territory. Alongside the Husayn-McMahon Agreement, there was the Sykes-Picot Agreement – a plan to carve up Syria and Mesopotamia (modern Iraq, Syria and Kuwait) between Britain and France – and in 1917 the Balfour Declaration promised to establish a national homeland for the Jews in Palestine. As Eugene Rogan says, with nice understatement, 'One of the challenges of British post-war diplomacy was to find a way to square what were, in many ways, contradictory promises'.[6] Historians still disagree on whether Lawrence was aware or not of these conflicting promises and, if he was, whether he was deliberately deceiving his Arab allies or if he hoped to create a momentum for independence that would be unstoppable, and whether his disenchantment at the end of the war was due to his guilty conscience, his anger at the British, or his disillusionment with the Arabists' surety of purpose. By the time of the Paris Peace Conference, it was clear that the Arabs were not to get their Independence.

Lawrence's legend grew after the war. The journalist Lowell Thomas, who had met him while covering the war for the American press, used a mixture of reportage, iconic photographs and film footage to create *With Allenby in Palestine and Lawrence in Arabia*, basically a touring slide show, but what we would now call a multimedia performance, with projections, incense burners, exotic dancers and military bands to amplify and extend his dramatic retelling of Lawrence's exploits. It was Thomas who invented the name 'Lawrence of Arabia'. The performances were hugely successful, filling the Royal Opera House in Covent Garden nightly from 14 August to 25 October 1919, after which it transferred to the Albert Hall, and then the Philharmonic Hall. It would eventually play to around four million people worldwide. (Rattigan's character of Franks, with his mythologising lantern lecture in Act One, Scene Three, is a clear reference to Thomas.)

Lawrence affected to dislike Thomas's performance, though he went to see it more than once, and contributed to his own growing mythology by writing *Seven Pillars of Wisdom*, his personal account of the Arab Revolt. It was first printed privately in 1922, before a slight abridgement was published in 1926 and a more substantial abridgement in 1927, under the title *Revolt in the Desert*. The book immediately impressed with its thrilling narrative and limpid, elegant prose; some of Lawrence's account has been verified and some of it disproved, but it did nothing to dampen excitement about his wartime exploits.

When Lowell Thomas described Lawrence as 'backing into the limelight', he was describing a man who did not seek fame, nor feel comfortable with it, and this impression was intensified when in December 1922, the *Daily Express* revealed that Lawrence of Arabia had enrolled in the ranks of the RAF, hiding his identity under the assumed name John Hume Ross. Forced out of the RAF for this deception, he was eventually admitted into the Tank Corps in July 1925, under the name 'Shaw', where he refused promotion and divided his time between the Corps, his cottage in Dorset, his motorbike, and his high-society friends (who did indeed include, as Ross declares in the play, 'Lord and Lady Astor, Mr and Mrs George Bernard Shaw, the Archbishop of Canterbury…' (p.15). As Liddell Hart, an early biographer, wrote of him in 1934, 'His one extravagance is motorcycling [...] To T.E. this sensation of supreme speed is entirely exhilarating, because it seems to free the spirit from the bondage of human weakness, and also, I think, because it suggests the power to overcome impediments that nature and human nature place in the way of all achievement'.[7]

This exhilaration would come to an end rather abruptly a year later when Lawrence was killed in a biking accident. There had been no diminution of interest in Lawrence by the time of his death. Indeed, as Liddell Hart's breathless prose suggests, Lawrence was beginning to be seen in some quarters as an almost superhuman figure, someone who might unite Britain, even Europe, as the threat of a new war loomed larger. His friend Henry Williamson wrote urging him to step into politics, declaring, apparently sincerely: 'You alone are capable of negotiating with Hitler'.[8] Churchill himself suggested later that 'I hoped to see him quit his retirement and take a commanding part in facing the dangers which now threaten the country'.[9] One sees lurking in such praise a feeling not merely that Lawrence might have been able to control Hitler, but that he might even have been Britain's equivalent of Hitler. Liddell Hart notes with bemusement that some were talking of him 'in a Messianic strain – as the man who could, if he would, be a light to lead stumbling humanity out of its troubles', before throwing caution to the wind himself and declaring Lawrence 'the Spirit of Freedom, come incarnate to a world in fetters'.[10]

His death only preserved his mystery. His letters were published in the late 1930s, and then *The Mint*, his own bawdy account of his time in the RAF, was published in 1955. Questions continued to surround him. What drove his action in the Holy Land? What did he actually do? Why did he withdraw afterwards? The question of his motives lies at the heart of *Ross* – 'Why are you really doing this?' asks Storrs (p.38) – and, during the run of the play, a biography of Lawrence appeared with these words on the cover: 'Legend or phoney? The battle of words goes on long after Lawrence's death'.[11]

That battle had been commenced in 1955, with the publication of Richard Aldington's *Lawrence of Arabia: A Biographical Enquiry*. Under that mild title lay a vehemently muck-raking biography which accused its subject of 'a systematic falsification and overvaluing of himself and his achievement […] In other words, the national hero turned out at least half a fraud'.[12] In addition to sharply diminishing Lawrence's significance to the Arab Revolt, the book also published for the first time claims that Lawrence was a homosexual, something Aldington plainly considers rather damning. In *Ross*, Aldington's views are represented by Barrington's unremittingly hostile judgements ('Awful little show-off – quite a bit of a sadist, too. Cold-blooded. No feelings. Doubt if his private life would bear much looking into, either' (p.33). The otherwise heroic movie *Lawrence of Arabia*, which opened in cinemas in December 1962, shows the influence of Aldington in its portrait of its hero's sadistic impulses.

In 1968, the *Sunday Times* published revelations that for the last thirteen years of his life, Lawrence had regularly hired a young man, John Bruce, to flagellate him on the buttocks, a story amplified in yet another biography, *The Secret Lives of Lawrence of Arabia*.[13] In the same year, in Alan Bennett's play *Forty Years On*, Lawrence and his mythology are the subject of satirical amusement: 'Shaw, or Ross as Lawrence then called himself, returned from the East in 1919. Shyness had always been a disease with him, and it was shyness and a longing for anonymity that made him disguise himself. Clad in the magnificent white robes of an Arab prince, with in his belt the short curved, gold sword of the Ashraf descendents of the Prophet, he hoped to pass unnoticed through London. Alas, he was mistaken.'[14]

Rattigan and Ross

The downfall in their reputation in the 1960s was not the only thing that connected Rattigan to Lawrence. Both of them were middle-class, Oxford-educated Englishmen who hid their personalities with obsessiveness and guile. When Ross is asked why he joined the RAF and replies 'I think I had a mental breakdown, sir' (p.10) – actually the reply Lawrence is reputed to have given[15] – one might be reminded of Rattigan's own decision to join the RAF in 1940 under the advice of his psychiatrist. More significantly, Rattigan's father was a diplomat and Terry spent some time as a young boy in Egypt where men who would become key figures in Lawrence's story, including Ronald Storrs, passed regularly through the family home. Rattigan was just the right age for the adventures of Lawrence of Arabia to captivate his childhood.

But it is hidden sexuality that chiefly connects the two men. Rattigan focuses on the moment in Deraa when Lawrence was captured, tortured and assaulted. While in *Seven Pillars of Wisdom* it is just another episode in the book, a moment of terrible suffering but one from which Lawrence claims to have recovered, for Rattigan it is the key to his personality and the turning point of the play. Put simply, Rattigan's Lawrence is a man in flight from his own homosexual masochistic desires: his decision to join the Arab Revolt is a sublimation of these desires, an attempt to conquer them through sheer force of will. But in Deraa he is forced to face them, and the revelation breaks him. Rattigan evidently felt that he had particular insight into Lawrence's psychology. What the Turkish General tells Ross after his assault sounds more like Rattigan addressing Lawrence: 'You must understand that I know... I know what was revealed to you tonight, and I know what that revelation will have done to you' (p.87). Rattigan could be emotionally cold himself, and in a later play he links sado-masochism to emotional repression through the phrase *'le vice Anglais'*.[16] The sadism that Lawrence displays after Deraa – especially in Act Two, Scene Six – might be paralleled with the emotional brutality with which Rattigan reportedly treated some of his former lovers.[17]

The decline of deference that is often associated with the 1960s in fact has its roots in the First World War. In the last six months of the war, Lytton Strachey published *Eminent Victorians*. Containing biographical sketches of four Victorian heroes and heroines, Cardinal Manning, General Gordon, Thomas Arnold and Florence Nightingale, the book was striking for discussing not merely their great achievements but dwelling wittily and irreverently on their flaws of character. One of the new duties of the biographer, Strachey declared, is 'to maintain his [sic] own freedom of spirit. It is not his business to be complimentary'.[18] It was a sign of a new prurient attitude to public figures and perhaps one of the reasons that Lawrence tried so hard to back out of the limelight. There is a cultural thread that connects Strachey to Aldington and perhaps too that lies in the reviews of Rattigan's previous play, *Variation on a Theme*, which began to make barely disguised references to the playwright's sexuality.[19] While Rattigan is not writing a personal apologia, there is an aspect of *Ross* that wants to explain, even justify, the effects of someone's private desires on their public behaviour.

For all these reasons, when Rattigan writes to Lawrence's brother in 1959, asking approval for the play, and speaking of 'my fervent sympathy with the subject', he is not just buttering up a useful ally. Rattigan felt a painful affinity with Lawrence and believed he possessed particular insights that justified his claim 'that of all present writers in the dialogue form I was the one best fitted to do justice to the memory of T.E.L.'[20]

The idea for a film, as opposed to a play, of Lawrence's life had been brought to Terry by his long-term film producer, Anatole 'Tolly' de Grunwald, in early 1955. Rattigan was enthusiastic, so Tolly bought the film rights for £3,000 to Liddell Hart's biography of Lawrence, hoping to circumvent the very protective Lawrence family. Rattigan spent much of 1956 researching, re-reading *Seven Pillars of Wisdom* as well as Lawrence's letters and biographies. The screenplay was sold to the Rank Organisation in February 1957 and a substantial budget of £700,000 was allocated to the project. Anthony Asquith was hired to direct, Dirk Bogarde to play the lead, and Tolly and Asquith began scouting possible locations in the Middle East.

The script that Rattigan submitted, *Lawrence of Arabia*, was never produced, for reasons that will become clear, but the script remains one of Rattigan's boldest and most interesting pieces of work. It is worth describing the script in some detail to give a sense of how it evolved into the stage play *Ross*. The screenplay begins at the end of an evening outside a country house; the guests are leaving and among the expensive cars is a motorbike, and one of the guests, Lawrence himself, leaves the party on it. He stops to help a couple whose car has broken down but he accidentally allows the crank handle to jerk back, fracturing his wrist. He suffers the pain in silence even on his return to the barracks. Already the screenplay is hinting at his curious affinity with private pain. ('I've an idea you don't like authority' says the Commanding Officer. 'I enjoy discipline,' replies Lawrence impishly.[21]) In the screenplay, unlike the stage play, while still an intellectual figure, Lawrence is a more confident participant in the all-male banter. As in the play he is confronted by his blackmailer and then has a malarial dream which seems to usher in a series of flashbacks.

But here in the screenplay his story is much more extensively told, beginning with Lawrence the Oxford undergraduate, declaring his intention to travel to Syria to research crusader castles. We see a montage of his travels before an Arab bandit tries to rob him. He disarms his assailant at first with wit as well as force but is eventually arrested and questioned. Kept in an old prison he meets Hamed, a member of Fetah, an Arab nationalist organisation, and they both escape using – slightly improbably – Lawrence's knowledge of Arabic architecture to figure out a weak point in the wall. After briefly returning to Oxford, he continues his archaeological explorations, filling the Ashmolean Museum with his finds. When war is declared he tries to enlist and is eventually accepted into the Intelligence Corps and posted to Cairo. Coming across a guest speaker briefing the senior officers on the Arab Revolt, he takes over the meeting, showing up the speaker's ignorance and arguing the Arab cause. Although seemingly in trouble for this impertinence, he is able to meet Abdullah, Sharif Husayn's son.

From this point, the screenplay broadly follows the outline of the play, though it is able to show more epic action from the dramatic – we see a good deal of Lawrence's sabotage of the Hejaz Railway – to the comic – his first encounter with Farraj and Daud (who will be called Rashid and Hamed in the play) comes when Daud is in trouble with Abdullah for spilling green paint all over his camel, at which point we see the surreally unlucky beast against the desert panorama. At the end of the play, Ross's real identity has been exposed by the press, and he is forced to leave. With Hamed's words 'God will give you peace' ringing in his ears, he sees an RAF plane zooming low overhead as he leaves the camp. '*Lawrence, laughing, pulls his goggles down over his eyes and accelerates his cycle to full speed, in a race against the airplane overhead.*'[22] It's a powerful image of hubristic heroism (foreshadowing the real Lawrence's death) in which Ross seems to be a figure uncertainly poised between earth and the heavens.

However, the film would not be made. Tolly and Asquith's attempt to find locations soon ran into difficulties. An initial hope to film in Jordan fell through when Glubb Pasha, the British Lieutenant-General who ran the Jordanian West Bank, was dismissed in March 1956 by King Hussein, who wanted to show that he was not controlled by the British. They then turned their attention to Egypt, hoping to film around Cairo, but in October the Suez Crisis put paid to that. They then turned to Iraq as a location, but this was a period of revived Arab nationalism and an alliance between Iraq and Jordan raised tensions that would lead to the assassination of King Feisal II (grandson of Lawrence's ally Feisal) in July 1958. Shooting costs were rising rapidly, and Rank began to lose faith in the project. On 14 March 1958, returning from yet another reconnaissance trip, Tolly and Asquith received the news at London Airport that Rank had pulled their funding from the project.

The news was devastating and potentially meant over two years of work lost. The high budget for the film meant it would be almost impossible to sell the script to another studio. So Rattigan decided to change direction, using the research to build a stage play instead. Although there would be somewhat cinematic elements to the final play, in fact the stage play is a complete rewrite and bears only a very general relationship to the screenplay: 'The screenplay, in fact, was little help to me,' Rattigan wrote. 'In some ways it was a hindrance.'[23] Rattigan worked on a draft of the stage play through the autumn and winter and finished it at 6 a.m. on 13 February 1959, sending it to his usual producer Hugh 'Binkie' Beaumont and then rewarding himself by going on several weeks of holiday, returning in May to find that Binkie was enthusiastic, asking for just a few cuts and rewrites. Glen Byam Shaw was brought on to the project as director. It was a good match: Shaw had directed the premiere of *The Winslow Boy* but had also in 1933 briefly met T. E. Lawrence ('I must introduce you two Shaws,' Sassoon had said).[24] Dirk Bogarde, about whom Rattigan had not been particularly enthusiastic, was replaced by Alec Guinness. Despite being a little old for the role – Lawrence was twenty-seven when the Arab Revolt began, and when the play opened Guinness was forty-six – he was an inspired choice: a contemporary of Rattigan, he shared the playwright's fascination with Lawrence: 'As a boy,' Guinness once declared, 'I was endlessly throwing a towel over my head and tying a tie round it and pretending to be Lawrence of Arabia'.[25] He had other affinities with Lawrence too, both being illegitimate, rather withdrawn, self-conscious characters, both privately homosexual.[26]

The first draft of the play is structurally very close to the final draft. Rattigan retained the screenplay's framing device of Ross in the RAF. Indeed the device is more insistent than in the final version, as we return to the Uxbridge Depot at the beginning of the second act. This is because Rattigan has decided, for this first stage draft, that the questioning of Lawrence's identity should be concentrated in Act Two[27] and the conversation that opens the second act is intended to open up this theme, though it does give the play an awkwardly broken-backed feel as well as bouncing us out of the wartime storyline just as it is getting interesting. This structure means that the first-act curtain line is less complex than in the published text. In this first draft, Ross, in his flowing Arab robes, has arrived in Cairo and informed the startled High Command that Akaba has been taken. Left alone on stage:

> *He rings off, and then leans back in the posture he adopted before.*

> [LAWRENCE] (*Quietly, at length.*) Why not – Lawrence – of Arabia?

> *Curtain.* [28]

The first act builds up the mythological identity; the second act breaks it down.

While Rattigan worked on redrafting and reshaping the material, another danger was looming in the form of the Lawrence family. When Binkie first approached the Lord Chamberlain, then charged with licensing plays for performance, he had been advised to contact the family to get their support for the performance. At this time, the Lord

Chamberlain was still very wary of permitting plays to be performed containing portraits of living or recently deceased public figures. Rattigan therefore wrote to Professor A.W. Lawrence, T. E.'s younger brother. Professing his deep sympathy with his subject and insisting on his wish to offer a positive portrait, he concluded, 'I thought you might need reassurance that, whatever my shortcoming as a "dramatic biographer", my heart, at least, is in the right place', and enclosing a draft of the play. Professor Lawrence was uncharmed by the playwright's overtures, responding: 'The "portrait" of T. E. Lawrence conveyed by the play to my mind is that of a weakling with a compensatory blood-thirst and other uncontrolled neurotic impulses.'[29]

Hoping to get more endorsements that might sway the family, two of Lawrence's friends were consulted. Siegfried Sassoon replied promptly and positively: 'My impression is that the play – with Alec G – would be very effective... The portrait of T. E. is, as you say, fully sympathetic and understanding. For me, it is always painful to read about what T. E. suffered in his interior life, but I welcome anything which defends him against the attacks which have been directed at his integrity. (He was a modern Hamlet).' Robert Graves, however, was less encouraging. In fact, since the collapse of the Rank film project, producer Sam Spiegel had begun to put together the team that would eventually make the epic *Lawrence of Arabia* (1962) and Robert Graves had been hired as a consultant, something he did not declare when he wrote to Binkie that he thought the play 'all right' but remarked, threateningly, 'one can't libel the dead but on the other hand one can be prevented from misrepresenting the dead by the copyright laws'.[30]

There then followed a complicated series of quadrilateral negotiations between Rattigan, Professor Lawrence, Liddell Hart and Robert Graves. Rattigan replied to Graves courteously, distancing himself from the *ad hominem* approach of Aldington: 'A.W. Lawrence's reactions seem to me perfectly understandable – although, as you'll appreciate – knowing so many parties concerned – it *is* a little hurting that Binkie B, Alec, Glen Byam Shaw, the Lord Chamberlain's Office and myself should all be considered as being involved in some dark conspiracy to dishonour the memory of T.E.L. – five Aldingtons, in fact, for the price of one – when, of course, our purpose is the exact opposite.'[31] Graves, unmoved, wrote to Professor Lawrence suggesting that he demand 'the removal of non-historical material where it misrepresents T. E. and the circumstances in which he found himself and also exact a promise that in the acting version no "business" is introduced that has the same effect'.[32] These would have been impossible constraints both on the writer and director, as Graves probably knew.

Liddell Hart offered to persuade Rattigan to correct the most egregious errors of fact, but Professor Lawrence realised that the facts were not the whole problem: 'Between ourselves,' he wrote, 'I should be more than satisfied if he cut out the passages in which "Ross" exults in slaughter & atrocities, & the mythical desertion; I can scarcely expect him to eliminate the popinjay-pansy talk since that would oblige him to rewrite all through so many scenes.'[33] Put simply, Professor Lawrence was reluctant to, as he saw it, play Rattigan's game, writing: 'I feel that R will wreck his play if he makes even a small proportion of the changes we'd want, & I'd rather he did not make token changes just to demonstrate his amenability – or to claim cooperation in a manner which might suggest it was genuine cooperation. The more *obvious* mistakes the better, I'd say, in matters of fact.'[34] While Liddell Hart acted as peacemaker, averring that *Ross* is 'a brilliant piece of work' and 'a powerful antidote to Aldington', Professor Lawrence was on the warpath: 'I may be wrong but my instinct at present is to await some move by the enemy before taking any action whatever.'[35]

The enemy did indeed take action, Binkie hiring the lawyer Peter Carter-Ruck, buying the stage rights to Liddell Hart's book for another £3,000 and a 1% royalty and putting together a dossier to show that they had attempted in good faith to gain the support of the Lawrence family, who were withholding it 'without good reason'. The Lord Chamberlain responded in October 1959 giving approval for the production, noting that a ban usually gave a play more publicity – and specifically drew attention to the controversial material – and that family feelings were difficult to protect, especially in the case of someone as much written about as Lawrence.[36] *Ross* could finally go ahead.

Ross in Performance

Alec Guinness was busy on another project and so rehearsals
didn't begin until the end of February 1960 at the YMCA off
Tottenham Court Road. It would be Guinness's first West End
role since he was knighted the year before, indeed his first theatre
role since *Hotel Paradiso* in May 1956, so the premiere was a
much-anticipated occasion. Several previews and interviews in
the *Daily Express*, *Daily Mail*, *Evening Standard* and *Guardian*
spoke warmly of Rattigan, agreeing, the first wave of enthusiasm
for the Angry Young Men having died down, that he had been
'too readily dismissed'.[37] Rattigan meanwhile continued to make
changes right the way through rehearsal, while also
simultaneously attending rehearsals in Covent Garden for *Joie de
Vivre*, which was due to open two months later.

Ross made unusual demands on the designer, with its multiple
locations and time jumps. Margaret Harris of the 'Motley'
design team went to Jordan with Glen Byam Shaw to get a feel
for the locations, very conscious that members of the audience
might be familiar with the locations from wartime experience or
commercial travel.[38] Design practices were, in any case, sharply
changing in 1960. The influence of some key European
theatremakers (and of Joan Littlewood's Theatre Workshop) had
pushed design in the direction of looser, more open, fluid and
flexible production styles, and this was reflected both in
Rattigan's dramaturgy, with its juxtapositions of scenes, its
specific use of lighting and sound to build the world of the play,
and in Margaret Harris's design. This featured a cyclorama
offering a blazing desert sky and a sand-coloured felt floorcloth,
tapered upstage to give the impression of endless desert.
Indicative flats were flown in to this basic set, and furniture
trucked on: for instance, the RAF office in Act One, Scene One
was represented by nothing more than a table and chair on a
wheeled platform, and a narrow flat suggesting a back wall. The
effect was almost Brechtian in its openness and simplicity.[39]
Music was commissioned from Na'im Al-basri, a prolific
composer for film and stage, who had, for example, composed
music for an adaptation at the Arts Theatre of Gide's *The
Immoralist* (another story of sexual self-discovery in North
Africa). The budget was set at £10,000, to which Rattigan

contributed £2,250 – more a sign of Terry's confidence than Binkie's lack.

The all-male cast was relatively inexperienced, certainly compared to Guinness, but featured a number of actors who would go on to play squarely establishment types in British theatre, film and television for the next half-century. Geoffrey Keen, for example, who played the Turkish General[40], would go on to play the Minister of Defence in several James Bond films. James Grout, cast as Franks, would play Inspector Morse's boss, Chief Superintendent Strange, in the 1990s. The blackmailing Aircraftman Dickinson was Gerald Harper, an actor and later DJ known for his smooth, romantic persona and the gimmick of sending roses and champagne to his female listeners. After a short pre-London tryout, the production opened at the Theatre Royal Haymarket on 12 May 1960. The company were not yet quite used to the epic style of the play, and there were some longueurs courtesy of the stage-management team, unused to so many set changes in an evening.[41]

The critics noted Rattigan's significant change in scale and ambition. The author, wrote W. A. Darlington in the *Telegraph*, 'set himself no mean task when he sat down to make a play about Lawrence of Arabia, one of the most extraordinary figures of our time. He has succeeded beyond expectation'.[42] *The Times*'s reviewer insisted that 'the dramatist has succeeded in bringing the character of his imagining to an intensely exciting stage life'.[43] J. C. Trewin in the *Illustrated London News* noted that 'Rattigan has always been an architect. But though I had long known his qualities, I had never imagined that he would write such a play as *Ross* which is among the most enthralling in years […] This is, believe me, an extraordinary night in the English theatre'.[44]

In speaking of the play's architectural qualities, Trewin is alluding to the elegance of its structure, something which did not find favour with all the critics. Robert Muller felt that 'Mr Rattigan's belief in craftsmanship is beginning to border on the obsessive now. The play is just too neatly balanced between the emotions, too immaculately constructed for the welter of material at his disposal'.[45] Bernard Levin in the *Daily Express*, while writing of the play quite warmly, was troubled by its 'smooth, pared, interlocking playmaking' and concluded that 'it is "only" Mr Rattigan's best play. But how nearly it is much, much more!'[46] Both of these responses are curious, given the play's open structure, its juxtaposition of elements, and its cascade of different devices (flashback, slide projection, dream play, chronicle structure). Indeed, it's one of Rattigan's least smoothly constructed plays, and perhaps these reviews suggest more the turning of the critical tide than an acute perception of the play's merits.

Lawrence's mysterious, fragmentary personality gave some critics trouble: ironically, the play that won the Evening Standard Award for 1960 was Harold Pinter's *The Caretaker*, perhaps the play above all others that persuaded audiences to accept partial and mysterious stage characterisation. But in 1960, few were prepared to accept this from Terence Rattigan: Milton Shulman felt that the play did nothing more to explain Lawrence's mystery than 'to punctuate the dot at the bottom of the question mark' (a phrase with which he must have been ever so pleased, given that he repeated it word for word in his review of the Old Vic revival twenty-six years later).[47] John Rosselli in the *Guardian* (in a review with the eyebrow-raising title 'Lawrence Remains Impenetrable') blamed the subject matter, feeling that 'something obdurate in Lawrence still fails to give a satisfying dramatic ring'.[48] Alan Pryce-Jones agreed: 'the Lawrence story is not really dramatic in stage terms. It needs glosses, hypotheses, even certainties'.[49] An audience today might find Lawrence's elusiveness precisely what makes the play dramatic.

But there was almost universal praise for Alec Guinness's portrayal. Anthony Cookman was enraptured: 'The exactness of his playing is a joy to watch, whether Lawrence is treating his military superiors with gentle intellectual patronage or is maintaining among the Arabs an air of aloof wisdom which masks his inner conviction that he is promising them more than his masters will later be prepared to pay.' Three months after the premiere, Robert Muller included Guinness's portrayal in a series of the great performances of the season. It is worth quoting his description at length as it gives a powerful sense of Guinness's achievement:

> As Aircraftman Ross, he suggests a man shorn of all arrogance, winded of all self-assertiveness, a man whose religion of

personal will has failed him through self-recognition. This is
the burdened Lawrence, living on the threshold of self-ending,
who holds, as it were, a protective pane of glass between
himself and his environment, between the Then and the Now.
Guinness plays Ross with a kind of elegiac compassion that
carefully sidesteps self-pity. His walk is inhibited, the hands
a little too solicitously held behind him. Painful shadows flicker
across his impassive face. His body quivers with spasms of
malaria and memory. When a callow young officer asks him,
Lawrence of Arabia, to look upon the officer as Dutch uncle
a ghostly grin haunts his mouth.

This contrasts with his transformation in the wartime scenes,
in which:

we see a fair, peacocky young man, dressing himself in
resplendent white robes before a mirror, a man who is part
mystic, part poseur, part self-mocking intellectual celebrating
the power of his will.

There were occasional dissenting voices, like Alan Pryce-Jones,
who felt that while 'there is not a single moment of his
performance which is not both calculated and intelligent
[… but] the calculation is too apparent'[50] (and Noël Coward,
who was bemused by Guinness's blond wig[51]). But most agreed
with Rosselli and Levin that Guinness was 'the inevitable and
only man for the part' and 'the only possible choice'.[52]

The production ran for two years, eventually racking up
762 performances at the Haymarket and making £342,663
in profit over the course of the run (around £7.5m in 2016).
A slimmed-down version of the show then embarked on a
regional tour for eight weeks. Even the Lawrence family were
happy. Professor Lawrence, who had hoped to disrupt the
opening with 'a blasting article or speech timed to coincide
with the first night', didn't see the show but judged from the
press coverage that Liddell Hart's influence had prevented his
first fears being realised.[53]

With the London production a success, plans were soon in hand
for a Broadway run. Binkie co-produced with New York
producer David Merrick. John Mills played the lead and
Geoffrey Keen was brought over to reprise his Turkish General.

The original sets were flown over and new ones made for
London. The production opened at the O'Neill Theatre on
26 December 1961. Some of the reviews were very positive:
Howard Taubman in the *New York Times* yoked it together with
Tennessee Williams's *Night of the Iguana*, which had also just
opened, as two plays that 'adorn the theatre by bringing to it
disciplined craftsmanship, distinction of style and integrity of
purpose'.[54] But from others it is clear that Lawrence exerted a
far less firm grip on the American psyche, with John Simon
remaining stubbornly uninterested in 'this series of loosely
connected unpenetrating vignettes'.[55] The production ran for a
respectable three months, transferring to a smaller theatre in
April, with the author waiving his royalties to keep it afloat for
a month, before closing in May.

The play has been revived less often than most other Rattigan
plays. In part, one might think, because it is expensive: it has
the largest cast – twenty-two – of any of Rattigan's major
plays[56], and its many, complicated locations make it a challenge
for the producers. The huge success of the film, too, has slightly
put the play in the shade, and the declining hold of the
Lawrence myth on the public imagination perhaps became a
disincentive soon after the play's premiere.

Ross was broadcast as Play of the Month on BBC1 on 18 October
1970, adapted by William Emms, with Ian McKellen as Ross and
Cedric Messina directing. The rest of the cast included Martin
Jarvis, Charles Gray, and Edward Fox. Otherwise, the play had
one professional revival in the fifty years after its premiere, at the
Old Vic in 1986, a production from the Theatre Royal, Plymouth.
Simon Ward played the lead, with David Langton as Allenby and
Bruce Montague as Storrs. Marc Sinden played Dickinson (his
father, Donald, had been in *Joie de Vivre* and his uncle, Leon
Sinden, had been Barrington in the first production of *Ross*).
Roger Redfarn directed. In 1960, the programme had included a
timeline of T. E. Lawrence's life but, emphasising the mystery of
his precise role in the Arab Revolt though also no doubt relying
on an audience's familiarity with the myth at least, the war years
were blank. In 1986, the programme had extensive articles on the
Arab Revolt and Lawrence himself, so far had these things faded
from public memory.

Rattigan's star was in its deepest eclipse in the mid-eighties. The reviews don't understand the play at all and don't even really try. Perhaps expecting an old-fashioned conservative play, they found one: *Ross* is referred to as a 'Boy's Own' story by *The Observer*, *Spectator*, *Daily Mail*, *Tablet*, and *Sunday Today*, which it really isn't.[57] Most of the reviews mock the play's coyness about homosexuality, and some of them rightly enough have little time for white actors blacked-up to play Arabs. Rattigan's stagecraft is mocked: 'The play rolls forward like a well-made juggernaut, exciting tears with killer efficiency.'[58] David Shannon in *Today*, however, found that 'it remains compassionate, funny and moving' and Julia Pascal in *City Limits* went further to suggest that 'the play works as a satirical historical drama that criticises English political double dealings'.

But that was all until 2016, when the play was revived at the Chichester Festival Theatre, in a production by Adrian Noble, starring Joseph Fiennes as Ross. At the same time, a new play, *Lawrence After Arabia* by Howard Brenton, opened at the Hampstead Theatre. Both productions were designed to mark the first centenary of the Arab Revolt. Britain's complicated relationship with the Middle East had become a much more pressing issue since 1986, and Lawrence's role had taken a different and more pertinent significance. For some Lawrence, with his love of Arab culture and history, had re-emerged in some quarters as a guide for western engagement in the region. During the Iraq war, US military leaders like General Petraeus took to quoting Lawrence's '27 Articles' from 1917 as a kind of counterinsurgency field manual. On the other hand, Britain's betrayal of the Arab nationalist cause in 1919 perhaps lay at the origin of tensions and resentments between the West and the East, and revisiting Lawrence's long nights in the Arabian desert might be a good way of understanding our own times.

Ross now

For these reasons, it may be easier to understand *Ross* now than it was even in 1960. A present-day audience is less troubled by a fragmentary, contradictory character. We are perhaps less likely to be thrilled by the mythology of Lawrence of Arabia and more keenly interested in the Arab Revolt itself. The episodic structure which plays with time and reality is far more familiar to us now than it was then. Lawrence's treatment at the hands of the Turks will seem more grimly familiar after the well-publicised use of rape as a weapon of war in Bosnia, Rwanda, and Darfur, as well as the sexual humiliation of male prisoners in Abu Ghraib prison. Lawrence's homosexuality and his sado-masochism is likely to be a less sensational and more sympathetic revelation than it could be over half a century ago.

The mystery of identity and desire is built into the riddling structure of the play. In its third scene, Aircraftman Ross is on his cot in an RAF hut, suffering from a resurgence of a malarial infection; as he sinks into fevered sleep, we see a kind of dream parody of Lowell Thomas's lantern lecture, with figures from Lawrence's past emerging to debate his character and actions. That dream clarifies to take us back to 1916 and Lawrence in the Arabian desert. What most critics did not understand is that we are still in Lawrence's dream and we remain so for most of the rest of the play. The play is more delirium than documentary. And we know this because of the various hallucinatory elements that weave unsettlingly through the play. At the end of the first half, Lawrence is left alone on stage in the British HQ in Cairo, and he soliloquises: 'Oh, Ross – how did I become you?' as the curtain falls. This is Ross in 1922 dreaming Lawrence in 1917 addressing Ross in 1922. It can only be a dream. Elsewhere we have Hamed speaking to Lawrence from beyond the grave, and even the opening moments, describing Lawrence's motorcycle accident, foreshadow his own death that would occur years after the events of the play.

The same might be said of the whole story of the Turkish General's actions. In Lawrence's own account, he is arrested by chance and brought to the district governor (the bey), fends off his sexual advances, and then is tortured and sexually assaulted before escaping. In Rattigan's version, the Turkish Governor knows that Lawrence has masochistic homosexual desires which his strong will is repressing, and plans to have him arrested and assaulted so as to confront him with these feelings and so break that will. Several commentators have poured scorn on this part of Rattigan's play. How could the Turks have known Lawrence's private sexual proclivities? How could they have been sure that to confront him with them would break his will? Is there any evidence the Turks even knew who their prisoner was? If they did, why would they have released him?[59] These questions melt away when we understand that the historical scenes are taking place in Lawrence's mind. In a sense, the Turkish General with his 'impossible' knowledge is a product of Ross's fevered introspection, not an historical figure at all. This chimes with some writers' sceptical handling of Lawrence's own account of the torture at Deraa: Nutting suspects the whole thing may be made up; Liddell Hart conversely thinks the significance of the episode was the discovery of ascetic self-denial; Aldington thinks Lawrence willingly submitted to the bey's sexual advances.[60] As Kaja Silverman writes 'it is impossible to know how much of this story has its basis in history, but in a way that is irrelevant. Fantasy has clearly intervened forcefully here'.[61] Rattigan's starting point, I suggest, is the same.

Silverman's sophisticated, nuanced, psychoanalytic reading of *Seven Pillars of Wisdom* shows how the European attitude to the Arabs, exemplified by Lawrence's book, confused Self and Other, in a mixture of homoeroticism and sado-masochism in a way that Rattigan would have recognised.[62] The pivotal torture scene in the play develops carefully over successive drafts to present something taut and shocking, yet ripe with ambiguity. Lawrence's own account is filled with sinister images of Oriental voluptuousness and vampirism, what Joseph Allen Boone had described as the stereotype of the 'cruel and effete Pasha'.[63] The bey is fat, sweaty, and effeminate, who dabbles his fingers in Lawrence's blood while cooing erotic promises at him.[64] At one moment the bey tells him, 'You must understand that I know',[65] which Lawrence is at a loss to interpret, but which becomes a key moment for Rattigan, suggesting a hallucinatory, almost psychic intuition.

In Rattigan's film script, the General is also a sensualist ('munching Turkish Delight' in one scene[66]) and offers the prisoner to his torturers as a kind of treat. We see him later descending the stairs and listening to the sounds of the torture with pleasure, smoking on a cigar.[67] The General enters, adds his own torment by burning Lawrence's skin with the cigar and, looking into his face, briefly seems to recognise who he is. After he leaves, the lieutenant who has been administering the beating admits that he hates the General, and ostentatiously drops a key, allowing Lawrence to free himself. There is no explicit reference to sexual assault: the General's line 'if he recovers, send him up to me. He rather interests me, this young man' might refer either to his suspicion that this is Lawrence or to a sexual motive.[68]

By the first draft of the play, the scene is recognisably that of the final, published version. The General is still the sensualist, drinking wine throughout the scene. His argument with the Captain is more extended than it would be in later drafts. One senses that Rattigan is still finding his way into the dramatic heart of the scene. The General's character is uncertain: he is partly arch-villain, crowing over his victim, and partly dinner-table wit (the Captain admits he doesn't understand and the General replies 'I know you don't, dear boy. You have a very obtuse mind. I've always said so',[69] slightly as if Noël Coward had spent time as a district governor in the Ottoman Empire). But the scene builds effectively towards the General's gloating confrontation of Lawrence with the truth of his own desires. And then, in a hangover from the screenplay that fits the character less well, he drops a key in front of his prisoner and leaves the room. The final moments of the scene are more detailed than they would be later: Lawrence grabs at a glass of water, makes his way painfully to his knees, and seems to try to take his own life with a blunt paper knife he finds on the General's desk, then by trying to break the water glass. Finally

> he picks up the key, and looks at it as if suddenly
> understanding its significance. He laughs suddenly, a
> cracked rasping sound, and with a tremendous effort gets
> to his feet. Staggering and swaying like a drunken man,
> with his knees barely supporting him, makes his painful
> way by inches towards the door that leads to the stairs.[70]

The scene is powerful but the suicide is uncertainly tied to Lawrence's character, and it seems strange that he takes so long to understand the key.

By the final draft, including some tweaks and cuts in rehearsal, the scene has been pared down significantly. The confrontation between the General and the Captain is down to the bare minimum, and everything is organised around the General's tauter, more elliptical face-to-face confrontation with Lawrence. The villainous wine drinking has also gone. Since the whole point of the General's plan is to release his captive with his mind shattered, he does not need to hint with a key; he simply tells Lawrence how to escape.[71] In successive drafts, therefore, Rattigan has intensified the action, stripped his treatment of the scene of its more overt Orientalist clichés, and pushed the play more towards the mental conflict with and within Lawrence.

The play is not, to be sure, free of the stereotypes of its era. It would be dangerous to claim that Rattigan's representations of Arabs had entirely escaped the ingrained Orientalism of his time and class, with all the patronising aspects that run through the mythologising of Lawrence of Arabia, but nor would it quite be right to say that there is nothing more to this than condescension. The first production's sensitivities to race may be judged by its crude stereotypes of Arabs played by white actors (it is bemusing to read a cast list in which a Turkish Captain is played by someone with as staunchly English a name as 'Basil Hoskins'). But the play internally tries to distance itself from the racism of its characters. Various British characters refer to Arabs as 'wog' and 'woggie' and are criticised for it. Rattigan characterises Barrington, one of the crudest racists in the play, as even less worthy of our admiration than the Turkish General. We might see the use of Orientalist clichés in the play – like the 1921 song 'The Sheik of Araby' – as drawing attention to the veils of illusion that intercede between the British and the Arab world.

To argue that much of the play takes place in Lawrence's dream is not to say that the whole play treats the story of the Arab Revolt as a backdrop for or emanation of Ross's purely personal anxieties. There is a reverberation between private desires and public policy. Images of narcissism and performance run through the play; the first time we see Lawrence in the desert he is trying on his Arab robes in front of a mirror: 'Storrs, how do I look?' he asks, with not a little campness (p.36). (It's even more so in the first draft: 'You know, Arthur,' says Lawrence, 'I simply love dressing up'.[72]) Our first image of the historical Lawrence is literally of a poseur. This is paralleled with the later scene, Act Two, Scene Five, which begins with the British senior staff having their photograph taken. An image persists through the play of British self-regard and self-interest.

To a contemporary audience, Lawrence's broken will may be an image of a British adventurer in the Middle East forced to confront his own delusions of power and influence. It is after this scene in the play that Lawrence loses faith in Britain's role in the Arab Revolt – 'the Arab Revolt is a fake, founded on deceit and sustained by lies, and I want no further part in it' (p.96) – a picture that reflects the historical Lawrence's own disillusion. In 1917, he left a famous note for his superior officer, announcing, 'I've decided to go off alone to Damascus, hoping to get myself killed on the way: for all sakes try and clear this show up before it goes further. We are calling them to fight for us on a lie, and I can't stand it'.[73] In one of the most moving and politically acute moments in the play, the loyal Arab bodyguard Hamed has heard rumours of the Sykes-Picot Agreement and quizzes Lawrence about it, who denies all knowledge. 'You could be lying to us,' says Hamed, not believing it. 'You could have lied to us from the beginning' (p.81). The play (unlike the David Lean film) makes clear that on some level, Lawrence *has* been lying, from the beginning.

Ross is not just a play about a crisis of sexuality but also a play about the bad conscience of the West. Aircraftman Ross's fevered dream is the nightmare of the West's tampering in the Middle East. When Lawrence comes to self-knowledge, he understands his and by implication Europe's complicated and unedifying mixture of sadism and masochism in their attitude to the Arab world. The myth of Lawrence of Arabia becomes a bad joke. The Arab scenes end with an image of horrified realisation, with Lawrence laughing at the pompous and small-minded Barrington until *'the laughter is no longer laughter, but the sound continues'* (p.110).

Notes

1. Robert Muller, 'Sir Alex is so splendid in Rattigan's so-neat play' *Daily Mail* 13 May 1960. All reviews of the 1960 production, unless otherwise stated, from Production File: *Ross*, Theatre Royal Haymarket, May 1960. V&A Blythe House Archive.

2. Quoted in Geoffrey Wansell, *Terence Rattigan: A Biography*, London: Oberon, 2009, p. 334.

3. At this time, the terms 'Ottoman' and 'Turk' were used interchangeably and I shall adopt this practice.

4. I am particularly indebted here to two excellent books by Eugene Rogan: his large-scale survey *The Arabs: A History*, 2nd ed., London: Penguin, 2011 and *The Fall of the Ottomans: The Great War in the Middle East, 1914-1920*, London: Penguin, 2015.

5. 'Sharif is spelled 'Sherif' in *Ross* which also has Feisal for the more current 'Faysal'. Indeed, different Arabic transliteration systems render names differently. Since I am using a great many different sources in this introduction, I cannot hope to reconcile all of these systems and there will be some inconsistencies in the spelling of certain Arabic names.

6. Rogan, *The Arabs: A History*, p. 187.

7. Liddell Hart, *'T. E. Lawrence' in Arabia and After*, London: Cape, 1934.

8. Quoted in Anthony Nutting, *Lawrence of Arabia: The Man & the Motive*, London: Trust, 1961, p. 234.

9. Quoted in Kaja Silverman, *Male Subjectivity at the Margins*, New York: Routledge, 1992, p. 309.

10. Liddell Hart, *op. cit.*, p. 448.

11. Nutting, *op. cit.* The word phoney appears in *Ross* in a description of one of the iconic images of Lawrence in the desert.

12. Richard Aldington, *Lawrence of Arabia: A Biographical Enquiry*, London: Collins, 1955, p. 8. The claims about Lawrence's homosexuality are throughout but given their fullest expression in part 3, chapter 6.

13. Philip Knightley and Colin Simpson, *The Secret Lives of Lawrence of Arabia*, London: Nelson, 1969.

14. Alan Bennett, *Plays: 1*, London: Faber and Faber, 1996, p. 56. The Headmaster's slide-show lecture may be itself a pastiche of scene 1.3 of *Ross*.

15. Liddell Hart, *op. cit.*, p. 417.

16. Terence Rattigan, *In Praise of Love*, edited by Dan Rebellato, London: Nick Hern, 2001, p. 94.

17. Michael Darlow records how Peter Osborn, a former partner, had reached out to Terry for friendship but was met by cold rejection (*Terence Rattigan: The Man and His Work*, London: Quartet, 2000, p. 360–361).

18. Lytton Strachey, *Eminent Victorians*, edited by John Sutherland, Oxford: Oxford University Press, 2003, p. 6.

19. See p. xv of this volume

20. Quoted in Wansell *op. cit.*, p. 317.

21. Terence Rattigan. *Lawrence of Arabia*. Undated manuscript [1957]. British Library. Rattigan Papers. MSS Add. 74396, p. 24.

22. *Ibid.*, p. 382.

23. Quoted in Wansell, *op. cit.* p. 318. The passage is from his initial letter to Lawrence's brother.

24. 'The Other Shaw' *Daily Telegraph*, 12 May 1960.

25. Quoted in Kevin Brownlow, *David Lean*, London: Faber & Faber, 1997, p. 418.

26. See Piers Paul Read, *Alec Guinness: The Authorised Biography*, London: Simon & Schuster, 2003, pp. 329–330.

27. See Wansell, *op. cit.*, p. 315.

28. Terence Rattigan. *Ross*. Undated manuscript [1959]. British Library. Rattigan Papers. MSS Add. 74402, p. 119. This manuscript is leather-bound and has the words TO A.G. FROM T.R.' stamped into the cover. It was a gift from Rattigan to Guinness on the opening night in 1960. Guinness later gave the manuscript to Simon Ward when the latter played Lawrence in the 1986 revival, before it ended up in the Rattigan Archive in the British Library.

29. Quoted in Wansell, *op. cit.*, p. 318.

30. Quoted in *ibid.*, p. 319. What Graves meant by this is not exactly clear, since if the play had drawn too much on either Graves's or Lawrence's own writings, it would be unlikely to have misrepresented Lawrence. In fact Spiegel had bought the right to Graves's *Lawrence and the Arabs* (1927) and to *Seven Pillars of Wisdom* and was probably waving his copyright around as a form of threat. Indeed, shortly after the play opened, Graves unwisely claimed that his copyright had been breached; Liddell Hart advised that the events mentioned were reported in many other sources than Graves's and Rattigan issued a stern telegram ('MY SOLICITORS HAVE BEEN INSTRUCTED TO ANSWER YOUR INSULTING INACCURATE AND DEFAMATORY COMMUNICATION' quoted in Fred D. Crawford, *Richard Aldington and Lawrence of Arabia: A Cautionary Tale*, Carbondale, ILL: Southern Illinois University Press, 1998, p. 151), after which nothing more was heard of the matter.

31. Quoted in Crawford, *ibid*, p. 146.

32. *Ibid*, pp. 146-147.

33. *Ibid.*, p. 148.

34. *Ibid.*, p. 147

35. *Ibid.*, pp. 148, 147.

36. Darlow, *op. cit.*, p. 359.

37. *Ibid.*, p. 363.

38. Michael Mullin, *Design by Motley*. Newark: University of Delaware Press, 1996, p. 178.

39. *Ibid.*, pp. 178-79.

40. Confusingly referred to as the Turkish Military Governor in the cast list.

41. Noël Coward noted in his diary 'There was a lot of scenic trouble which should *not* have occurred after four days of preparation. I think with Binkie's subtly decreasing interest in the theatre, the H. M. Tennent personnel are losing efficiency' (*The Noël Coward Diaries*, edited by Graham Payn and Sheridan Morley. London: Weidenfeld and Nicolson, 1982, p. 439.) See also Mullin *op. cit.*, p. 179.

42. W. A. Darlington, 'Guinness's Fine Study of Lawrence' *Daily Telegraph* 13 May 1960.

43. 'Ross Brought to Life' *Times* 13 May 1960.

44. *Illustrated London News* 28 May 1960. The review is unsigned but it is certainly Trewin's style.

45. Muller, *op. cit.*

46. Bernard Levin 'Rattigan builds Seven Pillars of Laughter' *Daily Express* 13 May 1960.

47. Milton Shulman 'After Ross... The Enigma of Lawrence Remains' *Evening Standard* 13 May 1960.

48. John Rosselli 'Lawrence Remains Impenetrable' *Guardian* 14 May 1960.

49. Alan Pryce-Jones. 'The Desert and the Despot' *Observer* 15 May 1960.

50. *Ibid*.

51. Coward, *op. cit.*, p. 439.

52. Both *op. cit.* This made it particularly tough for Michael Bryant who took over the role at the end of January 1961. The critics generally report him a decent replacement, more 'present', less intellectual than Guinness, but most agree with Philip Hope-Wallace that 'he does not exercise quite the same magnetism of the senior star player' ('Take-over bid at the Haymarket, *Guardian* 3 February 1961), though Harold Hobson is a dissenting voice, finding that 'He is less good than Guinness was in some episodes of Lawrence's career; in others he is actually better [...] What Mr Bryant does most brilliantly is to show the love, remorse, and spiritual terror which eventually made the maintenance of that [implacable] will a torment' ('These are for Connoisseurs' *Sunday Times* 5 February 1961).

53. Crawford, *op. cit.*, pp. 147, 150. He was soon distracted by the *Lawrence of Arabia* movie, whose script by Robert Bolt he seems to have disliked even more than Rattigan's.

54. Quoted in Susan Rusinko, *Terence Rattigan*, Boston: Twayne, 1983, p. 104.

55. Quoted in Wansell, *op. cit.*, p. 341.

56. Its all-male character list might also serve as a disincentive to directors interested in improving the gender balance of the stage.

57. Simon Ward, however, was well known for films of heroic deeds and swashbuckling derring-do, including *Young Winston* (1972), two Musketeers films (1973, 1974), *Aces High* (1976), *The Four Feathers* (1978), *Zulu Dawn* (1979). His casting may have misdirected the audience.

58. Mary Harron *Observer* 8 June 1986. All reviews can be found in *London Theatre Record* 6 (1986), p. 605-609.

59. Nutting states bluntly 'not only must this version be untrue; but it does not even make credible fiction' *op. cit.*, p. 115. It might be relevant to note that Nutting was also a paid adviser on the David Lean movie, and it was in his interests – as it was in Graves's – to disparage a rival treatment of the topic. However, Piers Paul Read also calls it 'far-fetched' (*op. cit.*, p. p. 330) and Milton Shulman in his review of Michael Bryant's debut in the role scorned the play's 'convenient manipulation of the facts so that they fit his theory', 'The new Ross – he may be nearer the truth' *Evening Standard* 2 Feb 1961. (Shulman was a convinced Aldingtonian)

60. Nutting *op. cit.*, p. 114; Liddell Hart, *op. cit.*, pp. 257-258; Aldington, *op. cit.*, p. 206.

61. Silverman, *op. cit.*, p. 329.

62. *Ibid*., pp. 299-338.

63. Joseph Allen Boone, *The Homoerotics of Orientalism*, New York: Columbia University Press, 2014, p. 96. This is to be contrasted with the contrary stereotype of the 'beautiful boy' (pp. 54–66) exemplified by Lawrence's characterisation of Daud and Farraj (Rashid and Hamed in *Ross*).

64. Lawrence, T.E. *Seven Pillars of Wisdom*. Stroud: Nonsuch, 2006, ch. 53.

65. *Ibid*., p. 311.

66. Terence Rattigan. *Lawrence of Arabia*. *op.cit*, p. 270

67. *Ibid*., p. 268. In the manuscript pp. 257–270 were reversed, for some reason, before being deposited with the British Library, which has a policy not to 'correct' such errors in archives (such 'errors' may somehow be significant to the archive).

68. *Ibid*. p. 266.

69. Terence Rattigan. *Ross*. *op.cit*, p. 163.

70. *Ibid*., p. 168

71. There are two more significant re-drafts of *Ross* in Rattigan's papers at the British Library: MSS Add. 74405 is a typescript with some manuscript additions, with some large cuts to the torture scene; MSS Add 74409 is the rehearsal draft, but even that, unusually for Rattigan, has some very extensive cuts and rewrites that were done during rehearsals.

72. Terence Rattigan. *Ross*. *op.cit*, p. 57.

73. Quoted in John C Hulsman, *To Begin the World Over Again: Lawrence of Arabia from Damascus to Baghdad*, Basingstoke: Palgrave Macmillan, 2009, p. 54.

List of Rattigan's Produced Plays

TITLE	BRITISH PREMIERE	NEW YORK PREMIERE
First Episode (with Philip Heimann)	Q Theatre, Kew, 11 Sept 1933 (transferred to Comedy Theatre, 26 Jan 1934)	Ritz Theatre, 17 Sept 1934
French Without Tears	Criterion Theatre, 6 Nov 1936	Henry Miller Theatre, 28 Sept 1937
After the Dance	St James's Theatre, 21 June 1939	
Follow My Leader (with Anthony Maurice, alias Tony Goldschmidt)	Apollo Theatre, 16 Jan 1940	
Grey Farm (with Hector Bolitho)		Hudson Theatre, 3 May 1940
Flare Path	Apollo Theatre, 13 Aug 1932	Henry Miller Theatre, 23 Dec 1942
While the Sun Shines	Globe Theatre, 24 Dec 1943	Lyceum Theatre, 19 Sept 1944
Love in Idleness	Lyric Theatre, 20 Dec 1944	Empire Theatre (as *O Mistress Mine*), 23 Jan 1946
The Winslow Boy	Lyric Theatre, 23 May 1946	Empire Theatre, 29 Oct 1947
Playbill (*The Browning Version* and *Harlequinade*)	Phoenix Theatre, 8 Sept 1948	Coronet Theatre, 12 Oct 1949
Adventure Story	St James's Theatre, 17 March 1949	
A Tale of Two Cities (from Charles Dickens, with John Gielgud)	St Brendan's College Dramatic Society, Clifton, 23 Jan 1950	
Who is Sylvia?	Criterion Theatre, 24 Oct 1950	
Final Test (TV)	BBC TV, 29 July 1951	

The Deep Blue Sea	Duchess Theatre, 6 Mar 1952	Morosco Theatre, 5 Nov 1952
The Sleeping Prince	Phoenix Theatre, 5 Nov 1953	Coronet Theatre, 1 Nov 1956
Seperate Tables (*The Table by the Window* and *Table Number Seven*)	St James's Theatre, 22 Sept 1954	Music Box Theatre, 25 Oct 1956
Variation on a Theme	Globe Theatre, 8 May 1958	
Ross	Theatre Royal Haymarket 12 May 1960	Eugene O'Neill Theatre 26 Dec 1961
Joie de Vivre (with Robert Stolz and Paul Dehn)	Queen's Theatre, 14 July 1960	
Heart to Heart (TV)	BBC TV, 6 Dec 1962	
Man and Boy	Queen's Theatre, 4 Sept 1963	Brooks Atkinson Theatre, 12 Nov 1963
Ninety Years On (TV)	BBC TV, 29 Nov 1964	
Nelson – A Portrait in Miniature (TV)	Associated Television, 21 Mar 1966	
All On Her Own (TV) (adapted for the stage as *Duologue*)	BBC 2, 25 Sept 1968	
A Bequest to the Nation	Theatre Royal Haymarket 23 Sept 1970	
High Summer (TV)	Thames TV, 12 Sept 1972	
In Praise of Love (*After Lydia* and *Before Dawn*)	Duchess Theatre, 27 Sept 1973	Morosco Theatre, 10 Dec 1974
Cause Célèbre (radio)	BBC Radio 4, 27 Oct 1975	
Duologue	King's Head Theatre, 21 Feb 1976	
Cause Célèbre (stage)	Her Majesty's Theatre, 4 July 1977	
Less Than Kind	Jermyn Street Theatre, 20 January 2011	

ROSS

A Dramatic Portrait

The author gratefully acknowledges his debt to
Captain B. H. Liddell Hart, both for the illumination afforded
by his book *T. E. Lawrence in Arabia and After* and for his help
in checking the script.

Dedicated with gratitude to
Anatole de Grunwald
who brought Lawrence to me and me to Lawrence

Ross was first presented by H.M. Tennent at the Theatre Royal, Haymarket, London on 12 May 1960, with the following cast:

FLIGHT-LIEUTENANT STOKER	Geoffrey Colvile
FLIGHT-SERGEANT THOMPSON	Dervis Ward
AIRCRAFTMAN PARSONS	Peter Bayliss
AIRCRAFTMAN EVANS	John Southworth
AIRCRAFTMAN DICKINSON	Gerald Harper
AIRCRAFTMAN ROSS	Alec Guinness
FRANKS (THE LECTURER)	James Grout
GENERAL ALLENBY	Harry Andrews
RONALD STORRS	Anthony Nicholls
COLONEL BARRINGTON	Leon Sinden
AUDA ABU TAYI	Mark Dignam
THE TURKISH MILITARY GOVERNOR	Geoffrey Keen
HAMED	Robert Arnold
RASHID	Charles Laurence
A TURKISH CAPTAIN	Basil Hoskins
A TURKISH SERGEANT	Raymond Adamson
A BRITISH CORPORAL	John Trenaman
ADC	Ian Clark
A PHOTOGRAPHER	Antony Kenway
AN AUSTRALIAN SOLDIER	William Feltham
FLIGHT-LIEUTENANT HIGGINS	Peter Cellier
GROUP CAPTAIN WOOD	John Stuart
Director	Glen Byam Shaw

Ross was revived at Chichester Festival Theatre on 3 June 2016, with the following cast:

FLIGHT-LIEUTENANT STOKER	Benjamin Wainwright
FLIGHT-SERGEANT THOMPSON	Brendan Hooper
AIRCRAFTMAN PARSONS	Gary Shelford
AIRCRAFTMAN EVANS	Rick Yale
AIRCRAFTMAN DICKINSON	John Hopkins
AIRCRAFTMAN ROSS	Joseph Fiennes
MOUTH ORGANIST	Christopher Walters
FRANKS	Nick Sampson
GENERAL ALLENBY	Paul Freeman
RONALD STORRS	Peter Sandys-Clarke
COLONEL BARRINGTON	Ian Drysdale
SHEIK AUDA ABU TAYI	Peter Polycarpou
TURKISH MILITARY GOVERNOR	Michael Feast
HAMED	Nicholas Prasad
RASHID	Eben Figueiredo
TURKISH CAPTAIN	Jay Saighal
TURKISH SERGEANT	Navinder Bhatti
KERIM	Jorell Coiffic-Kamall
ADC	Benjamin Wainwright
PHOTOGRAPHER	Brendan Hooper
FLIGHT-LIEUTENANT HIGGINS	John Hopkins
GROUP CAPTAIN WOOD	Nick Sampson

Director	Adrian Noble
Designer	William Dudley
Lighting Designer	Paul Pyant
Music	Mia Soteriou
Sound Designer	Paul Groothuis
Casting Director	Gabrielle Dawes

6

Characters

FLIGHT-LIEUTENANT STOKER
FLIGHT-SERGEANT THOMPSON
AIRCRAFTMAN PARSONS
AIRCRAFTMAN EVANS
AIRCRAFTMAN DICKINSON
AIRCRAFTMAN ROSS
FRANKS (THE LECTURER)
GENERAL ALLENBY
RONALD STORRS
COLONEL BARRINGTON
AUDA ABU TAYI
THE TURKISH MILITARY GOVERNOR
HAMED
RASHID
A TURKISH CAPTAIN
A TURKISH SERGEANT
A BRITISH CORPORAL
ADC
A PHOTOGRAPHER
AN AUSTRALIAN SOLDIER
FLIGHT-LIEUTENANT HIGGINS
GROUP CAPTAIN WOOD

ACT ONE

Scene One

Scene: an office. Behind a desk sits FLIGHT-LIEUTENANT STOKER. *He is an earnest, well-meaning young officer with a manner alternately avuncular and fierce.*

FLIGHT-SERGEANT THOMPSON *stands in front of him. He is an oldish man with a harsh rasping voice that inadequately conceals a soft heart for recruits and a contempt for all officers, including* FLIGHT-LIEUTENANT STOKER. *Standing at attention, in line, facing the desk, are three* AIRCRAFTMEN. *The centre man is* AIRCRAFTMAN PARSONS, *the accused. He is a tough ex-sailor of about thirty-five. He is without his cap. Of his escort,* AIRCRAFTMAN EVANS *is young and red-haired, and the other,* AIRCRAFTMAN DICKINSON, *is an ex-officer of the wartime Army in the ranks of the RAF for economic reasons.*

FLIGHT-SERGEANT (*to* PARSONS). Head up, you the accused. (*To the* FLIGHT-LIEUTENANT.) Aircraftman Parsons, sir.

FLIGHT-LIEUTENANT (*inspecting a charge sheet*). Three-five-two-one-seven-nine AC two Parsons?

PARSONS. Sir.

FLIGHT-LIEUTENANT (*reading from the charge sheet*). 'Conduct to the prejudice of good order and Royal Air Force discipline in that on December 16th, 1922, at the O-eight-three-O hours colour-hoisting parade the accused broke ranks and swore aloud.' (*Looking up.*) What's all this, Parsons?

PARSONS. Slammed my rifle butt on my toe, sir. Lifted my foot half an inch, sir. May have made a slight sound – but only to myself, of course, sir.

FLIGHT-LIEUTENANT (*to* FLIGHT-SERGEANT). Witness present?

FLIGHT-SERGEANT. I am the only witness, sir. I was drilling B Flight that morning.

FLIGHT-LIEUTENANT. Was the sound slight?

FLIGHT-SERGEANT. Rang across the parade ground, sir.

FLIGHT-LIEUTENANT. And was it – identifiable?

FLIGHT-SERGEANT. Very, sir.

FLIGHT-LIEUTENANT. I see. (*To* PARSONS.) You don't dispute that you swore?

PARSONS. No, sir.

FLIGHT-LIEUTENANT. Merely the volume?

PARSONS. Whisper, sir.

FLIGHT-LIEUTENANT. But it was heard clearly by the Flight-Sergeant.

PARSONS. Might have lip-read, sir.

FLIGHT-LIEUTENANT. It's still swearing on parade, isn't it?

PARSONS. Yes, sir.

FLIGHT-LIEUTENANT. And that's a serious offence. (*Looking down at the paper on his desk*). However, I'm glad to see it's your first. Still, that's not saying much after only ten weeks in the Service. (*To* FLIGHT-SERGEANT.) How is he at drill, generally?

FLIGHT-SERGEANT. He used to be in the Navy, sir.

FLIGHT-LIEUTENANT. Don't they order arms in the Navy?

PARSONS. Yes, sir. But they do it proper time.

FLIGHT-LIEUTENANT. Careful, Parsons.

PARSONS. Sorry, sir. I meant – different time.

FLIGHT-LIEUTENANT. Well, you'll just have to get used to the timing we use here at the Depot – which is, anyway, exactly the same as the Guards. Also to learn to order arms properly without hitting your foot and swearing.

PARSONS. Yes, sir.

FLIGHT-LIEUTENANT. Think yourself lucky I'm not putting this on your conduct sheet. Accused admonished.

FLIGHT-SERGEANT. Aircraftman Parsons and escort right turn, quick march.

PARSONS *and his escort march out.*

Right wheel. Left – right – left…

VOICE (*off*). Left wheel, mark time, halt. Right turn.

FLIGHT-LIEUTENANT. Next.

FLIGHT-SERGEANT. Sir. (*Marches to the door and opens it.*) March in.

VOICE (*off*). Escort and accused, attention, quick march, left…

LAWRENCE *and his* ESCORT *– the same as before – march in.* LAWRENCE *is now known as* AIRCRAFTMAN ROSS *and will, one day, be 'Shaw'. He is a small man of thirty-five with a long face and a sad, shy expression. He speaks in a very gentle voice.*

FLIGHT-SERGEANT. Left wheel, mark time, halt. Right turn. (*To the* FLIGHT-LIEUTENANT.) Aircraftman Ross, sir. (*Salutes.*)

FLIGHT-LIEUTENANT (*looking at the charge sheet*). Three-five-two-O-eight-seven AC two Ross?

LAWRENCE. Yes, sir.

FLIGHT-LIEUTENANT (*reading*). 'Conduct prejudicial to good order and Royal Air Force discipline in that the accused failed to report to the Guard Room by twenty-three, fifty-nine hours on December the 16th, 1922, on expiry of his late pass issued on that date and did not in fact report until O-O-seventeen hours on December the 17th. Period of unauthorised absence – eighteen minutes.' (*Looks up at the* FLIGHT-SERGEANT.) Witness present?

FLIGHT-SERGEANT. Guard commander's report, sir.

FLIGHT-LIEUTENANT (*looking at another document*). Oh yes. Well, Ross. Anything to say?

LAWRENCE. No, sir.

FLIGHT-LIEUTENANT. You admit the charge?

LAWRENCE. Yes, sir.

FLIGHT-LIEUTENANT (*looking at another document*). I see you've been on two charges already. Untidy turnout – three days' confined to camp; dumb insolence to an officer – seven days' confined to camp. So this charge makes the third in the ten weeks you've been in the Air Force. That's bad, Ross. That's very bad indeed. (*Suddenly thumps on the desk.*) Ross, I'm speaking to you. I said 'That's very bad indeed.'

LAWRENCE. I'm sorry, sir. I took it as an observation, not as a question. I agree, it's very bad indeed.

FLIGHT-LIEUTENANT (*after a pause*). I've an idea you don't care for authority, Ross?

LAWRENCE. I care for discipline, sir.

FLIGHT-LIEUTENANT. What's the distinction?

LAWRENCE. Very wide, I believe.

FLIGHT-LIEUTENANT. Being late on pass is an offence against both authority and discipline, isn't it?

LAWRENCE. Yes, sir. The point was academic.

FLIGHT-LIEUTENANT (*after a pause*). What made you join the RAF?

LAWRENCE. I think I had a mental breakdown, sir.

FLIGHT-LIEUTENANT (*more hurt than angry*). That kind of insolence isn't called for, Ross. I'm here not only to judge you but to help you. All right. Let's start again. Why did you join the RAF?

LAWRENCE (*slowly*). Because I wanted to, because I was destitute, because I enjoy discipline, and because I had a mental breakdown.

The FLIGHT-LIEUTENANT *stares at him, angrily.*

If you prefer, sir, we can substitute for 'mental' – the word 'spiritual'. I don't happen to like it myself, but at least it avoids the imputation of insolence.

FLIGHT-LIEUTENANT (*to* FLIGHT-SERGEANT). Flight?

FLIGHT-SERGEANT. Sir.

FLIGHT-LIEUTENANT. What is your report on this airman, in terms of general conduct?

FLIGHT-SERGEANT. Satisfactory, sir.

FLIGHT-LIEUTENANT. No signs of being bolshie – or general bloody-mindedness?

FLIGHT-SERGEANT. No, sir.

FLIGHT-LIEUTENANT. Drill?

FLIGHT-SERGEANT. Behind the others, sir, but he tries hard.

FLIGHT-LIEUTENANT. PT?

FLIGHT-SERGEANT. According to the sergeant instructor, sir, he has difficulty in keeping up with the squad, but then his physical handicaps come into that, sir.

FLIGHT-LIEUTENANT. Physical handicaps? This is a recruit, Flight-Sergeant, passed into the RAF as A-one. What physical handicaps are you talking about?

FLIGHT-SERGEANT (*uneasily*). Well, sir. I only know that twice after PT I've seen him being sick into a bucket, and he has some bad marks on his back, sir.

FLIGHT-LIEUTENANT (*to* LAWRENCE). What are these marks?

LAWRENCE. The scars of an accident.

FLIGHT-LIEUTENANT. A serious accident?

LAWRENCE. At the time it seemed so.

FLIGHT-LIEUTENANT. And you were passed as A-one?

LAWRENCE. Yes, sir.

FLIGHT-LIEUTENANT (*to the* FLIGHT-SERGEANT).
It seems very mysterious to me. (*To* LAWRENCE.) Where did you go last night?

LAWRENCE. To a place in Buckinghamshire – near Taplow.

FLIGHT-LIEUTENANT. By bus or train?

LAWRENCE. Motor-bicycle.

FLIGHT-LIEUTENANT. I see. Why were you late?

LAWRENCE. I fell off it.

FLIGHT-LIEUTENANT. Were you drunk?

LAWRENCE. No, sir. I only drink water.

FLIGHT-LIEUTENANT. How did you fall off?

LAWRENCE. I was going through Denham rather fast, but with a good ten minutes in hand, when a dog ran out into the street and I swerved. A car coming the other way hit me, and I was left with very little bicycle. It became necessary to run.

FLIGHT-LIEUTENANT (*after a pause*). When I asked you just now if you had anything to say in answer to this charge, you said 'no'.

LAWRENCE. Yes, sir,

FLIGHT-LIEUTENANT. You didn't think a motorcycle accident might be taken as a possible excuse?

LAWRENCE. No, sir. Only as a reason.

FLIGHT-LIEUTENANT. Another distinction?

LAWRENCE. Yes, sir. Another wide one.

There is a pause.

FLIGHT-LIEUTENANT. You think it's going to help your case if you impress me with the fact that you're an educated man. But that fact doesn't impress me at all – do you understand?

LAWRENCE. Yes, sir.

FLIGHT-LIEUTENANT. There are plenty of educated men in the ranks of the RAF. (*Looks suddenly from* LAWRENCE *to* DICKINSON.) You – escort – what's your name?

DICKINSON *very smartly steps a pace forward and stamps his foot in parade-ground manner.*

DICKINSON. Dickinson, sir.

FLIGHT-LIEUTENANT. I know something about you. You were at a public school, weren't you?

DICKINSON. Yes, sir.

FLIGHT-LIEUTENANT. Weren't you also an officer in the Gunners?

DICKINSON. Yes, sir. Captain. Wartime commission, of course.

FLIGHT-LIEUTENANT. At the front?

DICKINSON. Yes, sir. Passchendaele and the big Hun push in March '18. I got a 'blighty' there, sir.

FLIGHT-LIEUTENANT. And why did you join the RAF?

DICKINSON. I got a job when I was demobbed, selling motor cars, but I found I preferred Service life, sir. I consider the RAF the Service of the future and, when they turned me down for a commission, I decided to join anyway and work my way up through the ranks.

His answer has plainly pleased the FLIGHT-LIEUTENANT, *who nods smilingly at him.*

FLIGHT-LIEUTENANT. I hope you will. All right, Dickinson.

DICKINSON *steps back to his place beside* LAWRENCE *with supreme smartness.*

You see, Ross, this airman is in your Flight, and there are many others with similar records in other recruit squads. Where were you at school?

LAWRENCE. Oxford High School, sir.

FLIGHT-LIEUTENANT. Were you in the war?

LAWRENCE. Yes, sir.

FLIGHT-LIEUTENANT. In what capacity?

LAWRENCE. Oh – mostly – liaison work.

FLIGHT-LIEUTENANT. Liaison work? Where?

LAWRENCE (*after a slight hesitation*). The Middle East.

FLIGHT-LIEUTENANT. Where in the Middle East?

LAWRENCE. Oh, all kinds of places.

FLIGHT-LIEUTENANT. You seem very vague about it.

LAWRENCE. It was rather a vague kind of job.

FLIGHT-LIEUTENANT (*angrily*). For heaven's sake, man, you must have known what you were doing.

LAWRENCE. Not very often, sir.

FLIGHT-LIEUTENANT. When you talk about 'mental breakdown' you don't happen to mean just plain mad, do you?

LAWRENCE. Not certifiably so, sir.

FLIGHT-LIEUTENANT. You're in trouble of some kind?

LAWKENCE (*quietly*). Yes, sir.

FLIGHT-LIEUTENANT. Bad trouble?

LAWRENCE. It seems so, to me.

FLIGHT-LIEUTENANT. You mean when you tell other people they don't find it so bad?

LAWRENCE. I don't tell other people, sir.

FLIGHT-LIEUTENANT. No one at all?

LAWRENCE. No one at all.

FLIGHT-LIEUTENANT. If I sent the Flight-Sergeant and the escort out now – would you tell it to me?

LAWRENCE. No, sir.

FLIGHT-LIEUTENANT (*after a pause*). Look here, Ross, I'm not just your Flight Commander. You've got to try and look on me as a sort of Dutch uncle. (*After another pause.*) Well?

LAWRENCE. The untellable – even to a sort of Dutch uncle – can't be told.

There is a pause. The FLIGHT-LIEUTENANT, *frustrated, looks down at his desk.*

FLIGHT-LIEUTENANT. Why did you go to this place in Buckinghamshire?

LAWRENCE. To have a meal with some friends.

FLIGHT-LIEUTENANT. Close friends?

LAWRENCE. Some of them.

FLIGHT-LIEUTENANT. Give me their names.

LAWRENCE (*momentarily nonplussed*). Their names, sir?

FLIGHT-LIEUTENANT (*barking*). Yes, their names. (*Has taken up a notebook and pencil.*)

LAWRENCE. But have you the right...?

FLIGHT-LIEUTENANT. Yes, I have the right. (*Shouts.*) I want these people's names *now*. That's an order.

LAWRENCE (*with a faint sigh*). Very well, sir. Lord and Lady Astor, Mr and Mrs George Bernard Shaw, the Archbishop of Canterbury...

The FLIGHT-LIEUTENANT *has thrown his pencil down.*

FLIGHT-LIEUTENANT. All right! You now have two charges to answer – the present one and the one I'm putting you on tomorrow to be dealt with by the Group Captain, tomorrow, to wit – gross insubordination to your Flight Commander. On the present charge you get seven days' confined to camp. As for the second – well – I doubt if in future you're going to find much time to relax your troubled soul.

LAWRENCE. No, sir.

FLIGHT-LIEUTENANT. March him out, Flight.

FLIGHT-SERGEANT. Escort and accused, right turn, quick march.

LAWRENCE, DICKINSON *and* EVANS *march out. The* FLIGHT-SERGEANT *turns at the door.*

Right wheel. Left – right...

VOICE (*off*). Left wheel, mark time, halt. Right turn.

FLIGHT-SERGEANT (*closes door, turns*). That is the last charge, sir.

FLIGHT-LIEUTENANT (*wearily*). Thank God for that – (*Rises, looks at the day's orders on the noticeboard, then turns to the* FLIGHT-SERGEANT.) How's the Flight coming along generally?

FLIGHT-SERGEANT. About average, sir.

FLIGHT-LIEUTENANT. Think you'll make airmen of them?

FLIGHT-SERGEANT. Of a sort, sir.

FLIGHT-LIEUTENANT (*with a sigh*). I know what you mean. Shocking lot we're getting these days. But keep your eye on that chap Dickinson. I like the look of him. He ought to do well.

FLIGHT-SERGEANT. Yes, sir.

FLIGHT-LIEUTENANT. And give that cocky little bastard, Ross, hell.

FLIGHT-SERGEANT. Yes, sir.

He salutes magnificently, turns, stamping his feet as if to split his heelbones. The lights fade. In the darkness we hear the sound of a mouth organ playing and men's voices singing, softly and sentimentally, a popular song of the period 'The Sheik of Araby'.

Scene Two

Scene: part of a yard in the Depot. The afternoon of the same day. Enter MOUTH ORGANIST, *playing softly.* PARSONS, EVANS *and* DICKINSON *follow him on.* DICKINSON *is apart from the others, musing.*

EVANS (*to* PARSONS). No, listen, Sailor. After you were admonished, he asked him who he was out with last night and Rossie said, 'Mr and Mrs George Bernard Shaw and the Archbishop of Canterbury.'

PARSONS. Garn, Taff!

EVANS (*excitedly*). But he did, Sailor. I promise you he did.

PARSONS (*incredulously*). Archbishop of Canterbury? Rossie say a thing like that? Our Rossie? Oh no –

EVANS. But I was there, Sailor. I was escort. I heard him, clear as a bell. (*To* DICKINSON.) So did you, didn't you, Dickie-bird?

DICKINSON (*without moving*). What?

EVANS. When our officer – this morning said to Rossie, 'Look here, my man, I want you to tell me who you went out with last night' – what a bloody nerve to ask such a thing, mind you – did Rossie say Mr and Mrs George Bernard Shaw and the Archbishop of Canterbury?

DICKINSON. Yes. Also – Lord and Lady Astor.

EVANS (*triumphantly to* PARSONS). You see? You couldn't have done better yourself, Sailor. (*To* DICKINSON.) Weren't you proud of him, Dickie-bird?

DICKINSON. Not particularly.

PARSONS. Ex-ruddy-officer himself. Can't bear lip to one of his own kind.

DICKINSON (*quietly*). You know that's a bloody lie, Sailor.

PARSONS. Why weren't you proud of him, then?

DICKINSON (*without taking his eyes from the sky*). Because the Archbishop was enough. With the other names he overdid it.

LAWRENCE *comes in, staggering under the weight of a filled refuse bin.*

PARSONS. Hey, hey! And what do you think you're doing, Rossie, old bean?

LAWRENCE. There are still two left to fill.

PARSONS. Yes, Rossie-boy, that one and – (*Points off.*) and them there, left by my own instructions for a very good purpose, which is in case some bloody officer sticks his nose out here and says: 'I see you bleeders have done your fatigue, so you can bleeding well do another.'

LAWRENCE (*contrite*). I'm sorry, Sailor. I should have thought.

PARSONS (*kindly*). Yes, you should, shouldn't you? (*To EVANS.*) Ruddy marvel, isn't it? Reads Greek like it was the *Pink 'Un*, and don't know his bottom from Uxbridge Town Hall.

LAWRENCE *turns to pick up the bin.*

No, leave it there, for Gawd's sake. We don't want to have to fill it again. (*Helplessly.*) Cripes!

LAWRENCE (*flustered*). I'm sorry.

PARSONS. Never mind. Never mind. (*Suddenly thrusts out his hand.*) Rossie-boy –

LAWRENCE *turns and looks at* PARSONS' *outstretched hand in bewilderment.*

EVANS (*explanatorily*). The Archbishop.

LAWRENCE (*still bewildered*). The Archbishop?

PARSONS. And Mr and Mrs George Bernard Shaw, and in spite of what Dickie-bird says – Lord and Lady ruddy Astor – and though you might have added the Dolly Sisters and Gaby Deslys, still you can't think of everything, and I congratulate you, Rossie-boy. B Flight is proud of you.

He shakes hands with LAWRENCE.

LAWRENCE *is rather overwhelmed, and winces at the force of* PARSONS' *famous handshake.*

(*To the others*.) Salute our hero, boys.

There is a mild and faintly ironic cheer, and a few bars, also ironic, of a triumphal march from the MOUTH ORGANIST.

(*Puts his arm around* LAWRENCE*'s shoulder*.) Come and sing, Rossie. (*To the* MOUTH ORGANIST.) Give us the old Sheik again.

The MOUTH ORGANIST *plays*.

LAWRENCE (*timidly*). I'm afraid I don't know the words.

PARSONS (*shocked*). Cor stuff me! You must be the only man in England who don't. (*To* MOUTH ORGANIST.) Can you play anything in Latin or Greek?

LAWRENCE. I know 'Tipperary'.

PARSONS (*to the others, with irony*). He knows 'Tipperary'.

They all sing 'Tipperary'. PARSONS *leads the others, but softly, because of fear of discovery.* LAWRENCE*'s voice, rather quavering, can be heard, proving that at least he does know the words. They finish a chorus and* PARSONS *starts 'Pack Up Your Troubles'.* LAWRENCE *suddenly and brusquely breaks away from* PARSONS*' friendly embrace and moves quickly away from the group, his back to the others.* PARSONS *looks after him, rather surprised, but says nothing, continuing to sing. The* FLIGHT-SERGEANT *comes in past* LAWRENCE *who turns quickly from him.*

MOUTH ORGANIST. Here's the Flight.

The singing stops abruptly.

FLIGHT-SERGEANT. What's the idea of the concert?

PARSONS. We'd nearly finished fatigue, Flight.

FLIGHT-SERGEANT. Nearly isn't quite, is it? (*Points to the bin*.) What's that doing here? And how many more is there to fill?

PARSONS. Two, Flight.

FLIGHT-SERGEANT. Well, if you're smart and do 'em quickly I might find something else for you to do before supper. Jump to it now. Many hands make light work.

PARSONS. Oh. I wish I'd said that. How *do* you think of 'em, Flight?

FLIGHT-SERGEANT (*automatically*). None of your lip, Parsons, now – unless you want a dose of jankers.

LAWRENCE *picks up the filled bin.*

No. Not you, Ross. Evans – Dickinson, you take that. Rest of you inside, at the double. Ross, stay here.

EVANS *and* DICKINSON *take the bin from* LAWRENCE *and exit in the opposite direction from the others, who also exit. The* FLIGHT-SERGEANT *stares curiously at* LAWRENCE *for a moment.*

They been picking on you again, son?

LAWRENCE. No, Flight.

FLIGHT-SERGEANT. You don't ought to mind 'em so much.

LAWRENCE. I don't mind them, Flight.

FLIGHT-SERGEANT. Listen, I've got eyes in my head, haven't I?

LAWRENCE *lowers his eyes in embarrassment.*

LAWRENCE (*with a smile*). Flight, I'm sorry, but I'm afraid you've got it wrong. It was just that – suddenly – for the first time in five years I'd remembered what it was to feel life worth living.

EVANS *and* DICKINSON *enter,* EVANS *has his hands in his pockets.*

FLIGHT-SERGEANT (*barking*). Hands out of your pockets, you.

EVANS. Sorry, Flight. Can we go now, Flight?

FLIGHT-SERGEANT. No. Get a broom and sweep up those leaves over there. (*Points off.*)

DICKINSON *turns to make himself inconspicuous.*

And you, Dickinson.

The men murmur 'Yes, Flight' and exit. The FLIGHT-
SERGEANT *looks at* LAWRENCE *for a moment, frowning.*

Yes. You've got it bad, all right, haven't you? Real bad.
(*Smiling.*) Don't worry, I'm not young 'greaser'. I'm not
going to ask you what your trouble is.

LAWRENCE. Young 'greaser'?

FLIGHT-SERGEANT. Flight-Lieutenant Stoker to you. (*In
'officer' accent.*) 'I'm not just here to judge you, you know,
my man. I'm here to help you. Look on me as a sort of Dutch
uncle, old fruit.' Makes you bloody vomit.

LAWRENCE. It does, rather.

FLIGHT-SERGEANT. Mind you, I didn't say that and nor
did you.

LAWRENCE. No, Flight.

FLIGHT-SERGEANT. One day, if you want to tell me what's
up with you, you can and I'll listen. If you don't, that's all
right too. Meanwhile I've got to try and stop young greaser
from having you hung, drawn and quartered –

The men enter, carrying the two filled refuse bins.

(*To* PARSONS.) All right. At the double. And afterwards you
can dismiss. But don't let anyone see you or I'll personally
screw all your –

PARSONS. Ooh! Isn't our *Flight-Sergeant* the best little *Flight-
Sergeant* in the world? Say 'yes', boys, or it'll seem rude.
(*They cross and exit.*)

FLIGHT-SERGEANT (*shouting*). That's quite enough of that!
(*To* LAWRENCE.) All right. I'll do what I can. (*Suddenly
roaring.*) But don't ever let me hear you being insubordinate
to your Flight Commander like that again, do you hear?

LAWRENCE. Yes, Flight.

FLIGHT-SERGEANT (*to the corner, where* DICKINSON *and*
EVANS *have disappeared*). All right, you two. *Fini.* But
keep out of sight of any bleeding officer, if you please.

He exits. LAWRENCE *squats on the ground with his legs tucked under his body and takes out a small notebook and pencil and writes.* DICKINSON*, carrying a broom, and* EVANS *enter.* DICKINSON *puts the broom against a wall and languidly looks at* LAWRENCE.

EVANS (*approaching* LAWRENCE). Rossie?

LAWRENCE. Yes, Taff?

EVANS (*with acute embarrassment*). I wouldn't be asking this at all, but I thought perhaps – well – you're not the same as the rest of us and perhaps pay parade doesn't mean to you as much as it means to some of us, and...

LAWRENCE. I'm afraid it does, Taff. Quite as much.

EVANS (*overwhelmed with remorse*). Oh, but, then, please you must not on any account...

LAWRENCE. How much would it have been?

EVANS. Well, it was a ring you see – something I had to buy – you know – to make it up with my girl, you see, and she likes the best, always has – thirty-seven and six.

LAWRENCE. I wish I had it, Taff.

EVANS *looks over at* DICKINSON*, who, almost imperceptibly, shakes his head.*

EVANS (*with a sigh*). Oh well.

He exits sadly. LAWRENCE *continues to write in his notebook. Pause.* DICKINSON *approaches* LAWRENCE.

DICKINSON. Why do you sit like that?

LAWRENCE. I always do.

DICKINSON. It's the way the Arabs sit, isn't it?

LAWRENCE. I don't know.

DICKINSON (*squatting beside him*). But you should know – shouldn't you – after all that liaison work you did in the Middle East in the last war?

LAWRENCE. I'm sorry. I wasn't paying attention. Yes, it's the way the Arabs sit.

DICKINSON. Damned uncomfortable it looks. Why are you shivering?

LAWRENCE. I've got a touch of malaria.

DICKINSON. Middle East, I suppose? You're shaking quite badly. You'd better see the MO.

LAWRENCE. No. I'll have a temperature tonight and tomorrow it'll be gone.

DICKINSON. Yes, but you shouldn't take risks, old chap. After all, we don't want to lose you, do we?

LAWRENCE. I doubt if B Flight would notice.

DICKINSON. I wasn't talking about B Flight. I was talking about the nation.

LAWRENCE *puts down the notebook and stares steadily at* DICKINSON.

Well, aren't you going to say – 'What on earth do you mean?' Aren't you going to try and act it out just a little bit longer? (*Pauses.*)

LAWRENCE *stares at him steadily, but says nothing.*

I agree, old boy. Useless. At the same time I notice you're not falling into the trap of saying 'How on earth did you find out?' and so confirming what might, after all, be only a wild guess. Secret Agent training, no doubt. Very good. Well, old boy, it isn't a wild guess. It *was* until this morning, I grant. As a matter of fact I did see you once, in Paris, in 1919 – Peace Conference time – I was just a humble Captain, walking down a street and suddenly I found myself shoved back against some railings by some barmy gendarmes and practically crushed to death by an hysterical crowd because *you* were leaving your hotel. I couldn't see you well, but I remember you walking shyly – oh so shyly – between two policemen – to your car, head well down under that Arab headdress and then – at the car – turning to talk to someone so that the crowd grew even more hysterical, and then, when you were in the car, modestly pulling down the blind. Still, I wouldn't necessarily have recognised you, old boy, from that – nor even from the lecture I went to at the Albert Hall, which was supposed to be about the Palestine Campaign, but which had your picture on every other slide – very carefully posed, old boy, I hope you don't mind my saying – (*Offers a cigarette to* LAWRENCE.)

LAWRENCE *shakes his head.*

(*Lights one for himself.*) Still think I'm guessing? Look, old chap, it isn't awfully hard even for a humble airman like me – to find out the telephone number of Cliveden House, to ring up and ask if there'd been a raincoat left behind last night by Colonel Lawrence. 'Colonel Lawrence, sir?' Well-trained, this footman evidently. 'Yes, for heaven's sake – Colonel Lawrence – my dear man.' Slight pause. 'Oh, very well, then, Aircraftman Ross, if you like.' Another slight pause. Then, 'No, sir. The Colonel left nothing behind last night. In fact, I distinctly remember when he left that he had his raincoat strapped on to the back of his motor-bicycle.' (*Pauses.*) Your hand really *is* shaking badly, old boy. I honestly think you'd better see the MO. After all, you can't do punishment drill with malaria.

LAWRENCE (*in a low voice*). What do you want?

DICKINSON (*genially*). Money.

LAWRENCE. I haven't any.

DICKINSON (*murmuring*). Oh yes. 'Destitute.' I enjoyed that this morning.

LAWRENCE. It was the truth.

DICKINSON (*hurt*). Don't treat me like a halfwit, old boy. I'm not like the others. I can use the old grey matter, you know. I can tell how much money a man with your name could make for himself if he tried. Your memoirs? God! They'd make you a bloody fortune, and don't tell me you're not writing them, old boy, because I've seen you scribbling away in that notebook when you think no one's looking.

LAWRENCE. What I'm writing is for my friends. It's not for money.

DICKINSON. Jolly noble. Well, a bit of it had better be for money, old boy, because to keep my trap shut about this little masquerade of yours, you're going to have to pay me a hundred quid. That's what I reckon I could get from Fleet Street.

LAWRENCE *shakes his head.*

Listen, I haven't an earthly what you're up to, old boy, and I don't care either. Hiding? Spying? Having fun? Doesn't concern me. But it must be damned important to you that I don't give the story to the papers. So let's not haggle. Seventy-five, and I'll take a cheque.

There is a pause.

LAWRENCE (*presently*). No.

DICKINSON. You mean that?

LAWRENCE. Yes.

DICKINSON (*with a sigh*). Oh well, I thought you mightn't fork out. You were so damn careless with young greaser this morning, that I felt pretty sure you must have finished whatever it was you came into this thing to do.

LAWRENCE (*suddenly fierce*). I haven't finished. I haven't even started.

DICKINSON. What *did* you come into this thing to do?

LAWRENCE. To find peace.

There is a pause; then DICKINSON *laughs quietly.*

DICKINSON. Oh yes – the mental and spiritual breakdown.

LAWRENCE. Go and telephone the papers...

DICKINSON. Oh, I'm not ringing them up. This transaction's got to be strictly cash.

LAWRENCE. You'll go and see them?

DICKINSON. Yes.

LAWRENCE. When?

DICKINSON. Tonight.

LAWRENCE. Have you got a late pass?

DICKINSON. No. Just ways of egress and ingress.

LAWRENCE (*bitterly*). I see. Well, have fun tomorrow with the headlines.

DICKINSON. Don't tell me you're frightened of headlines, old boy.

LAWRENCE. I am now. Oh yes, you spotted my enjoyment of that crowd in Paris and this morning too – showing off to the Flight-Lieutenant, but forgetting all about the sharp-witted escort who was going to end my life –

DICKINSON. Suicide threat?

LAWRENCE. No, statement of fact. I mean my life as Aircraftman Ross.

DICKINSON. What does that matter? Lawrence will still be alive.

LAWRENCE (*with anger*). Lawrence doesn't exist any more. If you kill Aircraftman Ross you kill me. Can I put it more simply than that?

There is a pause.

DICKINSON. I don't scare very easily, you know.

LAWRENCE. I'm sure you don't. I wish I didn't.

DICKINSON. Are you being clever and acting this, old boy? (*Angrily.*) Why the hell is all this so important to you?

LAWRENCE. Why is a monastery important to the man who takes refuge in it?

DICKINSON. A monastery is for someone who's lost his will to live. (*Angrily.*) All right. The spiritual breakdown. I'll buy it. How did you lose your soul?

LAWRENCE. The way most people lose it, I suppose. By worshipping a false god.

DICKINSON. What god?

LAWRENCE. The will.

DICKINSON. The thing that's up in your head, you mean?

LAWRENCE. The thing that *was* up in my head.

DICKINSON. Isn't that what's made you what you are?

LAWRENCE. Yes.

DICKINSON. I meant Lawrence of Arabia.

LAWRENCE. I meant Ross of Uxbridge.

DICKINSON (*hotly*). Self-pity – that's all it is. There's nothing in the world worse than self-pity.

LAWRENCE. Oh, yes there is. Self-knowledge. Why shouldn't a man pity himself if to him he is pitiable? But to know yourself – or rather to be shown yourself as you really are… (*Breaks off.*) Yes. How stupid those Ancient Greeks were. With your public-school education I'm sure you'd understand what I mean. Can I borrow a couple of pounds?

DICKINSON *takes out his wallet and extracts two pound notes from it and hands them to him.*

Thank you. That proves it. You're going to do it.

DICKINSON. Good psychology. Yes, I'm going to do it, all right – because I'm damn well not going to be cheated out of money I need by a bit of fake playacting –

LAWRENCE. Aren't you confusing Ross with Lawrence? Or is Ross a fake too? Perhaps you're right. It doesn't matter much, anyway. Fake or not, he's been a dreadful failure. Lets the Flight down at drill and PT, can't tell a dirty joke to save his life and never sees the point of one, either, talks la-di-da and spoils any party by trying too hard. Still, just now, with Sailor and 'Tipperary' I thought it was just possible… (*Breaks off.*) No. That was sloppy thinking. Ross dies tomorrow and he'll be better dead – (*Looks dispassionately at his shaking hand, then up at* DICKINSON, *with a quick smile.*) Do you really think the papers will pay you a hundred pounds?

DICKINSON. More, perhaps.

LAWRENCE. Really? You will tell me how much they *do* pay, won't you?

He turns and exits. The lights fade. In the darkness we hear the distant sound of the 'Last Post'.

Scene Three

Scene: a hut at the Depot. The same night. There are four beds. PARSONS lies on one in his underclothes. He is working out racing results from an evening paper. EVANS lies on his bed, in his pyjamas. He is writing a letter.

PARSONS. Taff – what's six to four on, doubled with a hundred to eight against?

EVANS. Sorry, Sailor, I'm not a racing man. (*Bent over his letter.*) You tell me something.

PARSONS (*bent over his calculations*). What?

EVANS. Another word for love.

PARSONS *looks at him morosely without replying.*

(*Explosively.*) Love, love, love. Man, you get sick of it. I tell you. (*Waves the letter.*) Don't you know another word?

PARSONS. Who's it to?

EVANS. My girl. The one I'm marrying.

PARSONS. That minister's daughter?

EVANS *nods.*

I don't know another word.

EVANS. But she's different, you know, Sailor. Not at all what you'd imagine. Free-thinking, that's what she is.

PARSONS (*muttering*). Free-doing, too, I hope.

EVANS. You'd be surprised.

DICKINSON *enters and goes to his bed.*

PARSONS. Ah. Dickie-bird – you'd know. Six to four on, doubled with a hundred to eight against – in half-crowns?

DICKINSON. Let's see. Two-thirds of twelve and a half – roughly eight and a third. Two over three plus twelve and a half – thirteen and a bit. Twenty-one and a half to one double – two pounds, thirteen and threepence.

PARSONS (*admiringly*). Now that's the sort of brainwork I appreciate. (*Nods his head disparagingly towards* LAWRENCE*'s bed*.) I'll bet *you* don't read Greek poetry in the lats, Dickie-bird.

DICKINSON. You're damn right, I don't, old boy. The *Police Gazette*'s about my level.

LAWRENCE *enters and goes to his bed, passing* DICKINSON *as he does so.* DICKINSON *does not look at* LAWRENCE, *who removes his jacket with evidently rather uncertain fingers.* LAWRENCE *suddenly seems to remember something. He takes two pounds out of his trouser pocket, goes to* EVANS *and hands the notes to him.*

LAWRENCE. Have you got half a crown?

EVANS (*looking at the notes*). But you said you didn't have it.

LAWRENCE (*not looking at* DICKINSON). I managed to raise it.

EVANS. Oh Ross, you shouldn't have. Will he wait – your man?

LAWRENCE. I'm sure he will.

EVANS. For how long?

LAWRENCE. I should think – for eternity.

EVANS (*handing a coin to* LAWRENCE). Pay day after next you shall have it back. It's a promise. And one day I'll do the same for you.

LAWRENCE. That's all right.

EVANS (*returning to his letter*). Rossie – you'd know. Aren't there any other words for love, except love, in the English? Think of something to surprise her.

LAWRENCE. I'm not an expert.

EVANS. Try.

LAWRENCE. Tenderness, devotion, the communion of two spirits.

EVANS (*doubtfully*). A bit tame.

LAWRENCE. I'm sorry.

PARSONS (*who has been staring at* LAWRENCE, *frowning*). Hey. What's the matter with you?

LAWRENCE. Nothing,

PARSONS (*approaches* LAWRENCE). You're shaking like a ruddy shimmy dancer. The sweats, too. Got a dose of something?

LAWRENCE *does not answer.* DICKINSON *answers for him.*

DICKINSON (*quietly*). Malaria.

PARSONS. Malaria?

LAWRENCE. It's all right, Sailor. It's not catching.

PARSONS. I don't care if it is or it isn't. I'm the senior here and I'm not taking no chances.

LAWRENCE *continues silently to undress.*

(*Peremptorily.*) Put your things on again and go and report sick. Don't play 'silly bleeders' now. (*Thrusts* LAWRENCE*'s tunic towards him roughly, trying to manoeuvre his arm into the sleeve.*)

LAWRENCE (*quietly, but in a voice of sudden, unmistakable authority*). Take your hands off me.

PARSONS (*bewildered*). What you say?

LAWRENCE. I dislike being touched. (*Takes his jacket from* PARSONS, *and hangs it up*).

PARSONS. Listen, Ross. I'm telling you to report sick.

LAWRENCE (*still quietly, but with the same authority*). I'm not going to report sick. I'm going to sleep it off here. (*Lies down on the bed, half-undressed, shivering, and pulls the blanket over him.*)

PARSONS. I'm warning you, my lad, if you're not reporting sick tonight, you're doing your bleeding PT tomorrow morning – malaria or no malaria. *Compris?*

LAWRENCE (*half-asleep*). *Compris.*

PARSONS. Enjoy torturing yourself by any chance?

LAWRENCE. It's a fair comment, I suppose. Goodnight, Sailor. If I make too much noise in the night, wake me up.

PARSONS. I'll keep a boot handy. (*Defeated, he turns to* DICKINSON *who is still lying, fully dressed, on his bed.*) And what do you think you're doing? Going to sleep like that?

DICKINSON *gives him a lazy wink.*

What again?

DICKINSON *nods.*

Who is she tonight?

DICKINSON. No 'she' tonight. Business.

PARSONS. Funny time for business.

DICKINSON. It's a funny business.

PARSONS. Well, for God's sake, don't get caught.

DICKINSON. I won't.

PARSONS (*lowering his voice*). I'll expect the usual half-nicker.

DICKINSON. You might get a whole nicker if things go right.

PARSONS. I'll believe that when I see it.

The lights suddenly go out.

EVANS (*with a wail*). Oh no. Just when I'd got sort of inspired. I won't remember it tomorrow.

PARSONS. What?

EVANS. A time we were together one night on a beach
near Rhyl.

PARSONS. You'll remember it tomorrow.

EVANS. Not the words I was using –

PARSONS. You'll be remembering some other words if you
don't put a sock in it.

EVANS. But the words were good, Sailor –

PARSONS. Pipe down, you sex-mad Celt. Night, all.

EVANS *and* DICKINSON. Night, Sailor.

After a moment of silence and near-darkness, DICKINSON
*quietly gets up from his bed and moves on tiptoe towards the
door. He stops a second by* LAWRENCE*'s bed and looks
down. Then he tiptoes on.* LAWRENCE *suddenly flings out
his arm in a pleading gesture.*

LAWRENCE (*murmuring*). No. No...

DICKINSON *stops and turns back.*

DICKINSON (*in a whisper*). Speaking to me, old boy?

There is no answer, save a faint moan. It is plain that
LAWRENCE *was talking in his sleep.*

Happy dreams, Colonel –

*He tiptoes to the door and exits. Blackout. After a pause we
hear a muffled roll of drums and the opening bars of 'Land
of Hope and Glory' played by an organ, but coming
apparently from a distance. When the lights come up we find
that a large magic-lantern screen has been lowered, on
which is a photograph of* LAWRENCE *in spotlessly white
Arab dress, with a large, curved, ornamental dagger around
his waist. He is lying on the ground, a rifle by his side,
gazing thoughtfully into space. A camel squats sleepily
behind him. The desert background looks decidedly unreal
and the whole effect is phoney and posed. In front of the
screen is a lecturer,* FRANKS, *in a dinner jacket with a
billiards cue as a pointer.*

FRANKS. Ladies and gentlemen. This is the man. The Colonel himself – perhaps the most legendary figure of modern times – the scholar – soldier – the uncrowned King of the Desert – wearing, as you see – (*Points to* LAWRENCE*'s dagger.*) the insignia of a Prince of Mecca – an honour awarded him by Prince Abdullah...

LAWRENCE. No! No! No!

FRANKS (*testily*). Surely this is what you always wanted?

LAWRENCE. No longer. Now I only want you to tell them the truth.

FRANKS. But what is the truth?

A man whom we are later to meet as ALLENBY *appears from the darkness beside* FRANKS.

Ah – Field-Marshal? What was your view of Lawrence?

ALLENBY. Well, I was never too sure how much of a charlatan he was. Quite a bit, I should think. Still, there's no disputing the greatness of what he did.

RONALD STORRS, *a civilian in tropical clothes, has become visible.*

FRANKS. And you, Mr Storrs?

STORRS. I think the importance of what he did has perhaps been exaggerated – by the press, by people like you and – to be fair – by himself. It's in what he *was* that he was great – in my view, probably the greatest Englishman of his time.

BRIGADIER-GENERAL BARRINGTON, *in tropical uniform appears.*

FRANKS. Ah! General. You knew Lawrence, didn't you?

BARRINGTON. Oh, very well. Couldn't bear him. Awful little show-off – quite a bit of a sadist, too. Cold-blooded. No feelings. Doubt if his private life would bear much looking into, either. As for what he did – well, a lot of chaps did just as well, but didn't get the publicity.

The SHEIK AUDA ABU TAYI, *an old man of great vigour with a booming voice, a handsome hawk-like face and a natural unassumed majesty of presence, stalks on, shouldering* BARRINGTON *contemptuously out of the way.*

AUDA (*thunderously*). Tell them in England what I – Auda Abu Tayi – say of el Aurans. Of Manhood – the man. Of Freedom – free. A spirit without equal. I see no flaw in him.

LAWRENCE (*agonisedly*). No flaw?

AUDA. I see no flaw in him.

He exits. The TURKISH GENERAL *approaches the screen, but remains silent, looking towards the hut.*

FRANKS. You see how difficult it is. Where is the truth? They can't all be right, can they? I really think it's safe to stick to the simple story – that boy-scout epic of yours. You're a legend, you see – and I mustn't spoil it for the public. They want Lawrence, not Ross. They want a world hero, not a fever-stricken recruit, sick of life, sick of himself, on the threshold of self-ending. (*To the* TURKISH GENERAL.) Who are you? Are you part of the great Lawrence story?

GENERAL. Not of the legend. But I'm part of the truth. (*Behind* LAWRENCE*'s bed, looking down.*) But don't worry, my friend. I won't tell. I never have and I never will.

LAWRENCE. One day I will.

GENERAL (*politely*). Will you indeed? I never denied your bravery. But that would really be *very* brave – (*Exits.*)

FRANKS (*relieved*). That's enough of that unsavoury nonsense. Next slide, please.

A large map of the Middle East, pre-1914 war, is flashed on to the screen.

In 1916 the whole of this vast area – (*Points.*) was under the domination of the Turkish Empire, with which the Allies were at war. (*Points again*). The Turks were menacing the Suez Canal, and the British were too weak to attempt a counteroffensive. The great battle of the Somme had just cost them nearly half a million casualties, with no result. The whole vast war had bogged down in a morass of blood – and there seemed no way for either side to win. However, on June the 5th, 1916, an event occurred down here – (*Points to Mecca*.) on which the newspapers barely deigned to comment, although it was later to change the world's history. The Sherif of Mecca revolted against the Turks, captured their garrisons at Mecca and Jeddah, and with his sons the Princes Feisal and Abdullah and, with his tiny force of Bedouin tribesmen, challenged the might of the vast Turkish Empire. Disaster, of course, would have followed, but on October the 16th, 1916, there landed at Jeddah – (*Points*.) two Englishmen – one a mature, clever and far-seeing diplomat – Ronald Storrs – and the other – next slide, please –

A photograph of LAWRENCE *is flashed onto the screen. He is in the uniform of an Army Captain and looking sternly and soulfully straight into the camera lens.*

– a young man – filled with an implacable devotion to the cause of Arab unity, and a stern sense of duty to his own country.

LAWRENCE *laughs gently.*

What's the matter?

LAWRENCE. You make it all sound so dull.

FRANKS. Dull?

LAWRENCE. Yes. It wasn't like that at all. Not in the beginning. It was fun.

FRANKS (*sternly*). Fun, Aircraftman Ross?

LAWRENCE. Yes. In the beginning…

The lights fade. There is the sound of Arab martial music, jaunty and barbaric, but not at all stern and military. Interposed are the sounds of shouting and laughter.

Scene Four

Scene: the interior of an Arab tent. As the lights come on,
LAWRENCE *is being helped into an imposing-looking white*
Arab gown by a ferocious-looking, plainly disapproving Arab
servant (HAMED). *Another servant* (RASHID), *younger and*
gentler-seeming than the first, holds a mirror for LAWRENCE
to look into. STORRS *sits on a stool, smoking a cigar. The Arab*
music continues.

LAWRENCE (*surveying himself*). Storrs, how do I look?

STORRS. The most Anglo-Saxon Arab I ever saw.

LAWRENCE. In Syria, before the war – when on
archaeological jaunts – I used to pass as a Circassian.

STORRS. May I remind you we're about a thousand miles
south of Damascus. Have you ever heard of a Circassian
in the Hejaz?

LAWRENCE (*still distracted by his appearance*). No. I can't
say I have. Still, *one* might have wandered –

The music ceases.

The parade must be over. Just as well. I told Abdullah his men
were shooting off far too many bullets that should be kept for
the Turks. If I can't say 'Circassian', what *shall* I say?

STORRS. If I were you I'd say you were an English Intelligence
Captain on leave from Cairo, going on an unauthorised visit to
Prince Feisal's headquarters, through country that no Christian
has ever crossed before. They can't possibly believe you and
so all they may do is to make a small incision in your skull to
let the devil of madness out. It hurts quite a lot, I believe – but
at least there's a chance of survival –

LAWRENCE. Don't you think I need something round the
waist?

STORRS. What sort of something?

LAWRENCE. I don't know. Some sort of ornament. A dagger
for instance. I'm supposed to be dressed as a great lord of the
desert, you see. Abdullah thinks that the more conspicuous

I look, the less attention I'll cause, which is rather sensible –
don't you think? (*To* HAMED.) Go to the Lord Abdullah and
beg him in the name of Allah to lend to his servant Captain
Lawrence a dagger that would befit a Prince of Mecca.

HAMED *stares angrily at him for a moment, then turns,
and goes.*

He seems to do what I tell him, which is a comfort. I hope
the others do –

STORRS. What others?

LAWRENCE. Abdullah also wants me to take some of his own
men to reinforce his brother –

STORRS. Now I put your chance of survival at zero. The
minute they're out of sight of Abdullah's camp they'll slit
your infidel throat.

LAWRENCE. That's what Abdullah thinks too. (*Begins to
walk up and down.*) A sheik walks differently from ordinary
mortals.

STORRS (*unhappily*). I ought to stop you from going.

LAWRENCE. You can't, and well you know it. I don't come
under you.

STORRS. Seriously, my dear fellow, the risks are out of all
proportion to any good you think you can do. Oh yes – I know
it'll be fun for you if you get back to Cairo to infuriate the
senior officers by telling them that they've got their facts all
wrong – that you've inspected the situation at first hand and
know. But I honestly don't think you will get back to Cairo –

LAWRENCE. When I was an undergraduate I wanted to write a
thesis on crusader castles. So I went to Syria alone, without
money, in the height of summer, and walked twelve hundred
miles in three months. I was completely dependent on the
Arab laws of hospitality. People said then they didn't think
I'd get back to Oxford –

STORRS (*impatiently*). This isn't Syria. This is their Holy
Land. Down here the Arab laws of hospitality don't extend to
Christians. It's their religious duty to kill you –

LAWRENCE. Ah – but I have a bodyguard – don't forget.

STORRS. A bodyguard? You mean that thug over there – and his murderous-looking friend –

LAWRENCE. Oh, I don't think Rashid is a thug. I even got him to speak to me. He spat afterwards, of course, to clean his mouth, but in quite a polite way. I admit I haven't yet had the same success with Hamed, but I won't give up trying.

STORRS *gets up suddenly and goes up to* LAWRENCE.

STORRS (*touching his arm*). T. E.

LAWRENCE *withdraws his arm quickly.*

You might easily get killed.

LAWRENCE. I might easily get run over by a staff motor in Cairo.

STORRS. Why are you really doing this? (*As* LAWRENCE *opens his mouth.*) Don't tell me any more about that mysterious kinship you feel with the Arab race. I don't believe it. You don't love the Arabs. You happen to speak their language and get on with them, but you're not a mystic like Burton or Doughty. You're doing this for some very personal reason. What is it?

LAWRENCE (*after a pause and speaking with far more weight than his words*). I need air.

Before STORRS *can reply,* HAMED *comes in with an ornamental belt and dagger which he brusquely hands to* LAWRENCE.

(*With a winning smile.*) May Allah bless you, Hamed, friend of my heart and guardian of my life –

HAMED *turns his back and walks away with great dignity to stand beside* RASHID.

(*Shrugging.*) Oh well. Everything takes time. (*Showing* STORRS *the dagger.*) I say, Storrs – look at this. Isn't this splendid? (*Puts the dagger on, with apparent glee.*) Rashid, hold the mirror up again.

RASHID *does so*.

With this I shall really be one of the toffs of the desert –

BARRINGTON *comes into the tent, dressed in tropical uniform. He looks hot and bad-tempered.* STORRS *rises with alacrity.*

BARRINGTON. Storrs?

STORRS. Ah, hullo, Colonel. It's good to see you again.

BARRINGTON. I'm sorry I wasn't on the quay to meet you. The message from HQ about your arrival came late. How did you find your way to Abdullah's camp?

STORRS. Captain Lawrence found some man to guide us –

BARRINGTON. But that's very dangerous, you know, out here – strictly against regulations, too. And who's Captain Lawrence?

STORRS (*helplessly*). He's over there.

LAWRENCE (*turning, affably*). How do you do. You're Colonel Barrington, aren't you, our representative in Jeddah.

BARRINGTON. Yes. I am.

LAWRENCE. Tell me, what do you think of Abdullah?

BARRINGTON (*bewildered*). What do I think of His Highness? Well, I think he's an exceptionally able and gifted person –

LAWRENCE. Exactly. He's too able and gifted to see anything except defeat. I don't blame him for that, but I don't think he's really our man – do you? I'm putting my money on Feisal.

BARRINGTON. Are you?

LAWRENCE. Ah. You probably see Feisal as a fool because he thinks he can win, and, of course, if he merely thinks that, then, I agree, he is a fool. But if – just by some strange chance – he happened to believe it, then – well, he'd be our man, wouldn't he? It seems to me worth a trip, anyway. Excuse me, but I really must make use of as much daylight as possible. Hamed, Rashid, tell the men to make ready and mount.

HAMED *and* RASHID *disappear silently.* LAWRENCE *turns to* STORRS.

Well, goodbye, Storrs. I'll see you in about a month.

BARRINGTON. Are you intending to ride to Feisal? Is that the meaning of this rig-out?

LAWRENCE. It is a bit peculiar, isn't it? At first Abdullah wanted to disguise me as a woman, with a yashmak, but I thought that was going a bit too far. Also – sort of cheating too, don't you think?

BARRINGTON. Do you happen to realise the risks involved?

LAWRENCE. Oh yes. We've been into all that.

BARRINGTON. But do you know anything about the sort of country between here and the Wadi Safru?

LAWRENCE. A bit rough, I'm told.

BARRINGTON. Are you? Well, this is what *I'm* told. Bare desert without any shelter at all, for three days. Then four days climbing a virtually impassable range of mountains, another two days climbing down it, and then another three days across an even worse desert. Then –

He breaks off. LAWRENCE *is counting up on his fingers.*

What are you doing?

LAWRENCE. You've already made it twelve days. Quite frankly, Colonel, I'll be disappointed if we don't do it in six –

He goes out.

BARRINGTON. Who on earth *is* that awful little pipsqueak?

STORRS. Lawrence? My super-cerebral little companion? He's from the Arab Bureau in Cairo –

BARRINGTON. Ah, he's one of *that* menagerie, is he? Why was he sent out here?

STORRS. He wasn't. He just came.

BARRINGTON. Good Lord. Unauthorised?

STORRS *nods*.

What's his job in the Arab Bureau?

STORRS. Making maps.

BARRINGTON. Fine lot of use that's going to be to him.

STORRS. I don't know. His maps are very good.

BARRINGTON. Very artistic, I've no doubt – with the desert a tasteful yellow, and the mountains a pretty shade of mauve. (*Angrily*.) Listen, Storrs – I don't want to have anything to do with this business. I know nothing about it whatever – do you understand?

STORRS. Yes. Very clearly.

BARRINGTON. From now on Captain Precious Lawrence of the Arab Bureau is entirely on his own –

STORRS. Yes, I think he'd prefer it that way.

The lights fade. We hear the sound of a man singing an Arab song, quietly, from a distance.

Scene Five

Scene: a desert place. There is no feature except a rock against which LAWRENCE *reclines, writing in a notebook. The rest is sky and a burning sun. Beside* LAWRENCE *lies* RASHID, *flat on his back.* HAMED *is asleep, some distance away. The singing continues.*

LAWRENCE. What music is that, Rashid?

RASHID. It is the music of an Howeitat song, el Aurans, in praise of Auda Abu Tayi. (*Spits surreptitiously.*)

LAWRENCE. A noble man. They do well to honour him.

RASHID (*surprised*). Even in Cairo they know of Auda? (*Spits again*.)

LAWRENCE. Even in Cairo *I* know of Auda. Seventy-five blood enemies killed by his own hand, and all his tribesmen wounded in his service at least once. Assuredly the greatest warrior in all Arabia. (*Wistfully*.) What an ally he would make to Feisal!

RASHID. The Turks pay him too much money. He is a great man but he loves money. How is it you know so much about our country and our people, el Aurans? (*Spits again*.)

LAWRENCE (*mildly*). Rashid, for the last five days I have wondered much whether Allah might not forgive you if, in conversation with me, you saved everything up for just one great spit at the end?

RASHID. Don't tell Hamed or he will beat me. He is angry that I speak to you at all.

LAWRENCE. Your guilty secret will be safe, I swear.

RASHID. Answer my question, then, el Aurans.

LAWRENCE. How do I know so much about your country and your people? Because I have made it my business to learn.

RASHID. Why do you, an Englishman and a Christian, seek to serve our cause?

LAWRENCE. Because in serving your country I also serve my own. Because in serving your cause I serve the cause of freedom. And in serving you I serve myself.

RASHID. The last I don't understand.

LAWRENCE. I don't quite understand it myself. (*Gets to his feet*.) The hour is nearly finished. In ten minutes you must rouse the others.

RASHID (*groaning*). Oh no, el Aurans. The sun is still too high –

LAWRENCE. We must reach Prince Feisal's camp tonight.

RASHID. You will kill us all. For five days we have had no rest. Look at Hamed there. (*Points to the sleeping* HAMED.)

Never have I known him so weary. And I, I am a dying man, el Aurans.

LAWRENCE. Resurrect yourself, then, corpse. (*Playfully prods him*.) Are you, Bedouins of the desert, to be put to shame by a man who, until a week ago, had spent two years of his life astride an office stool in Cairo? I am ashamed to lead so weak and effeminate a band –

RASHID, *smiling, staggers to his feet, overplaying his weariness*.

RASHID (*with a giggle*). Who was it who yesterday had to hold you on your camel – to save you from falling down that ravine through weariness?

LAWRENCE. It was you, Rashid, and I thank you. But I would not have fallen.

RASHID. Allah would not have saved you.

LAWRENCE. No.

RASHID. Who then?

LAWRENCE. The only god I worship. (*Taps his head*.) It lives up here in this malformed temple and it is called – the will. (*Looking at* HAMED.) Surely Hamed will kill me for bringing him from such a happy dream.

RASHID. Let him dream on, el Aurans. And let me join him. (*Sinks to the ground in pretended exhaustion*.)

LAWRENCE (*gently*). You are with him in everything else, Rashid, I think at least you should allow him the solitude of his own dream. And it can only last another seven minutes.

RASHID (*pleadingly*). El Aurans, why not wait until the evening? What do five hours matter?

LAWRENCE. They can make the difference between winning and losing a war.

RASHID. A war? (*Pityingly*.) Forgive me, el Aurans, but I am an Arab and you are an Englishman and you do not understand. For five days I have heard you talk of an Arab war, but there is no war. We fight the Turks because we hate them, and we kill them when we can and where we can, and then when we have killed we go home. You speak of the Arab nation – but there *is* no Arab nation. My tribe is the Harif, and our neighbours are the Masruh. We are blood enemies. If I kill a Turk when I might have killed a man of the Masruh, I commit a crime against my tribe and my blood. And are the Harif and the Masruh the only blood enemies in all Arabia? How then can we be a nation, and have an army? And without an army, how can we fight a war against the Turks? When you speak of the Arab war you dream foolish dreams, el Aurans –

LAWRENCE. Very well. I dream foolish dreams. (*Looking at his watch.*) Five minutes and we leave.

RASHID (*disgusted*). To give Prince Feisal these few men when with a thousand times their number he could not storm the Turkish guns that face him at Medina. Is that the only purpose of this mad gallop that is killing us all?

LAWRENCE. No. Not to give Feisal a few men to help him storm Medina, but to give him one who will stop him from trying to storm it at all.

RASHID. Yourself?

LAWRENCE *nods*.

You will not persuade him. He believes in his madness he can drive the Turkish armies from all of the Hejaz.

LAWRENCE. And so do I, Rashid, and I am not mad.

RASHID. By Allah, I think you are madder. How can he drive the Turks from the Hejaz and not attack their fortresses?

LAWRENCE. Precisely by not attacking their fortresses, Rashid.

RASHID. And so he will win his battles by not fighting them?

LAWRENCE. Yes. And his war too – by not waging it.

RASHID. It is a splendid riddle, el Aurans.

LAWRENCE. The answer is easy, Rashid. It lies all around you. You have only to look. (*Points to the horizon.*) What do you see?

RASHID. Empty space.

LAWRENCE (*pointing again*). And there – what do you see?

RASHID (*shrugging*). Our camels.

LAWRENCE. Desert and camels. Two weapons that are mightier than the mightiest guns in all the Turkish armies. The two weapons that can win Feisal his war – if only we are in time to stop him destroying his army and his own faith and courage against the guns of Medina.

The sound of a shot, followed by confused shouting, coming from close at hand. HAMED *wakes and stretches.*

(*To* RASHID.) See what that is. Tell the men to save their energies for the ride, and their ammunition for the Turks. Get them mounted.

RASHID *runs off.*

(*Pushing* HAMED *with his foot.*) Leave your dreams, Hamed. It is time to go.

HAMED *looks up at* LAWRENCE *bewildered, and then quickly jumps to his feet and draws his revolver.* LAWRENCE *takes the revolver from him.*

If this pistol could speak it would surely say: 'See how my guardian reveres me. He keeps me spotless and gleaming, and ready for my master's use.' (*Returns the revolver to* HAMED.) Is that not so, Hamed?

HAMED, *for answer, abruptly spits quietly on the revolver where* LAWRENCE *has touched it and polishes it with his sleeve.*

(*Sighs.*) May Allah give us a short war and not a long one, or your lack of conversation may grow oppressive by the end.

HAMED *looks quickly at him.*

(*Cheerfully.*) Yes, Hamed. By the end. I mean to ask Prince Feisal to appoint you and Rashid permanently as my personal bodyguards. So the only way you will ever gain your freedom from my service will be to ask me for it, and without a spit to follow it.

HAMED *appears to pay no attention to news that is plainly unwelcome. He picks up a cartridge belt that* RASHID *had left behind.*

He is safe, Hamed. I sent him on an errand –

RASHID *runs on quickly. He looks startled.*

(*To* RASHID.) Well?

RASHID (*breathlessly*). Mahmoud the Moroccan has killed Salem of the Ageyli. Salem had insulted Mahmoud's tribe, and Mahmoud took his rifle and shot him as he lay asleep. Now the men of the Ageyli have bound Mahmoud and will leave him here for the vultures when we go.

LAWRENCE (*quickly*). And the other Moroccans? Where are they?

RASHID. Guarded by the Ageyli, each with a rifle to his back. They can do nothing, el Aurans. There are two Ageyli to each one of them.

LAWRENCE. And the rest of the men?

RASHID. They say it is no concern of theirs. Perhaps they will listen to you, el Aurans, but they would not hear me.

There is a pause. LAWRENCE *looks at the ground in thought.*

LAWRENCE (*at length, quietly*). Yes, Rashid. They must listen to me. I am their leader.

HAMED *spits.* LAWRENCE*'s eyes meet his.*

(*Raising his voice slightly. To* HAMED.) They are soldiers in the field, and I lead them. If Mahmoud has committed murder then he must be killed. But – (*After evident difficulty in forcing the thought into speech.*) by me – and not by them.

RASHID. They will not allow that, el Aurans. The Ageyli must kill him themselves, or their honour will not be avenged,

LAWRENCE. And the honour of the other Moroccans? How will that be avenged when they no longer have Ageyli rifles in their backs? You know well enough, Rashid, and so do I.

And then another Moroccan will die. And another Ageyli. No. *One* life for *one* life – (*Looks at his pistol and abstractedly fingers it.*) If they wish, the Moroccans can avenge their honour by killing me. Then it is only a Christian who dies and there will be no blood feud. (*Looking at his pistol.*) Once with this I could hit a matchbox at twenty yards. I wonder now if I can kill a man at one.

He turns to go. RASHID *and* HAMED *make to follow him.*

No. Stay here.

He goes out. The lights fade. In the darkness we hear first the sound of confused shouts and cries and, at a moment, growing much louder. Then there is a quick silence, broken by a voice crying suddenly, in agonised fear: 'Have pity, el Aurans. Give me mercy. Let me live!' Then comes a pistol shot followed at uncertain intervals by two more.

Scene Six

Scene: the Turkish Headquarters. A large wall map of the Hejaz Railway is being studied by the TURKISH GENERAL *and a* TURKISH CAPTAIN. *An* ORDERLY *stands by, holding notebook and pencil.*

GENERAL (*pointing at the map*). The latest report then puts him about here.

CAPTAIN. Further east. Here. Nearer to Wadi Sirhan.

GENERAL. But that's over a hundred miles from the railway. Are you sure that's correct?

CAPTAIN. It was confirmed by our agents.

GENERAL. When was his last raid on the railway?

CAPTAIN. Ten days ago at kilometre 1121. (*Points to a place on the map.*) He blew up the line in three places.

GENERAL. And nothing since then?

CAPTAIN. No. Perhaps our railway patrols are getting too hot for him.

GENERAL. The history of the last few months would hardly support that rather optimistic hypothesis. But why has he gone east away from Feisal? (*Turns away from the map. To* ORDERLY. *Peremptorily.*) Take this down. (*Dictating.*) 'Proclamation. To all loyal inhabitants of Southern Arabia. For some time past the criminal activities of a British spy, saboteur and train-wrecker, named "Lawrence", sometimes known as "el Aurans", "Laurens Bey" or the "Emir Dynamite", has been causing severe damage to Arabian property, notably the Holy Railway route from Damascus to Medina. In addition, his acts of wanton destruction pose a severe threat to the supplies of our garrison at Medina. A reward, therefore, of ten thousand pounds will be paid – '

CAPTAIN (*looking up, surprised*). For a figure like that we'll need authorisation from Damascus.

GENERAL. I'll write to them. (*Continuing*). '…will be paid to any person giving information leading to his capture. By order of the Military Governor, District of Deraa.' (*Gives* ORDERLY *a gesture of dismissal.*)

The ORDERLY *exits.*

CAPTAIN. Isn't that rather expensive for a terrorist?

GENERAL. For a terrorist. But not, I think, for Lawrence.

CAPTAIN. What's the difference?

GENERAL. The difference between a nuisance and a menace.

CAPTAIN. Menace? (*Scornfully.*) The Emir Dynamite?

GENERAL (*turning to the map*). The Emir Dynamite seems to be skilled in other things than high explosives. Strategy for instance. I don't think ten thousand is too much for a man who, in a few months, has transformed a local disturbance into a major campaign – who has isolated Medina – (*Points to the map.*) and who has drawn down – (*Points to the area of the Hejaz and Southern Arabia.*) into Southern Arabia, reinforcements from all over the Turkish Empire which are needed elsewhere. (*Abstractedly*.) Oh no. For this man I think ten thousand's rather cheap. (*With sudden excitement*.) Near to the *Wadi Sirhan*? Isn't that what you said?

CAPTAIN (*at the map*). Yes. (*Points*.) Here.

GENERAL. But, of course. Auda!

The lights fade as the sound of Auda's Battle Song can be heard being sung to Arab musical accompaniment.

Scene Seven

Scene: outside AUDA'*s tent. The sound of a song is coming from somewhere in the distance.* LAWRENCE, *in Arab clothes, is squatting on the ground with eyelids lowered.* RASHID *comes in quickly and speaks in a low voice.*

RASHID. El Aurans, there is danger.

LAWRENCE *raises his head slowly, as if interrupted in some process of thought.*

Hamed has just heard that the Turks have lately been to this camp and were received with great friendliness.

LAWRENCE *looks at him vaguely, his thoughts evidently elsewhere.*

(*Desperately*.) El Aurans, all Arabia knows this man loves money and takes it from the Turks. Hamed says we should leave at once.

LAWRENCE. Then he should come and tell me so himself.

RASHID. You know well he cannot. (*Giggling*.) And now he has made it even harder to break his silence to you. He has bound himself by the holiest vow he knows.

LAWRENCE. Well – at least that shows he feels temptation.

RASHID. Oh yes. He is tempted.

LAWRENCE. Hamed's must surely be the most prolonged
religious sulk in world history.

RASHID (*urgently*). We have the camels ready, el Aurans.
We can leave now.

LAWRENCE (*quietly*). No, Rashid. Not yet. I will tell
you when.

AUDA *enters from the tent, studying a map with intense
concentration.* LAWRENCE *nods to* RASHID *who exits
quickly.* AUDA *lowers the map and glares at* LAWRENCE.

Well?

AUDA (*at length*). No. It is impossible.

LAWRENCE. Since when has Auda Abu Tayi been turned back
from any venture by the dull bonds of possibility?

AUDA. El Aurans, it is only a few hours that I have known you,
but I understand you better than you think I do. You have
said to yourself, 'Auda is an old man who feeds on flattery.
All I need to do to bend him to my will is to remind him of
the great feats of his youth.' (*Suddenly shouting.*) Of course
there was a time when I ignored the word impossible. There
was a time, forty years ago, when I led a hundred men across
the Southern Desert against ten times that number to avenge
an insult to my tribe – and by the great God, avenged it too.
That day I killed seven men by my own hand.

LAWRENCE. Seven? In the 'Ballad of Auda' it says ten.

AUDA (*carelessly*). No doubt some others died of their
wounds. Yes, by heaven. That feat was impossible. And
there were others too – (*Changes tone.*) But I am no longer
twenty and what you suggest is – (*Shouting, off, angrily at
someone offstage.*) Kerim! Order that man, on pain of
instant decapitation, to stop singing his foolish song. The
words are exaggerated and his voice disturbs our thought.
(*Turns back to* LAWRENCE.) There exists a boundary
between the possible and the impossible that certain
exceptional beings such as myself may leap. But there is
a boundary between the impossible and a madman's dream
– (*The singing stops abruptly.*) Thank Allah! There are

fifty-six verses to that song – each in praise of either one of my battles or one of my wives. By the dispensation of God the numbers are exactly equal.

LAWRENCE. Wouldn't it be supremely fitting to the memory of a great warrior if his wives were outnumbered by just one battle – and that one the greatest of all?

AUDA (*passionately*). El Aurans, I have no great love for the Turks. Feisal is my friend and I would be his ally. But what are you asking? A march in the worst month of the year across the worst desert in Arabia – el Houl – the desolate – that even the jackals and vultures fear – where the sun can beat a man to madness and where day or night a wind of such scorching dryness can blow that a man's skin is stripped from his body. It is a terrible desert – el Houl – and terrible is not a word that comes lightly to the lips of Auda Abu Tayi.

LAWRENCE (*mildly*). I had believed it a word unknown to him.

AUDA. My friend, your flattery will not make wells. And it will not stop the few wells there are on the fringe of that desert from being poisoned by the Turks the moment they learn of our objective – as they must –

LAWRENCE. Why must they?

AUDA. Do you think I am unknown in Arabia? Do you think that when Auda rides out at the head of five hundred men the Turks will not ask questions?

LAWRENCE. Indeed they will, but will they get the right answer?

AUDA. They are not fools.

LAWRENCE. No. And that is why the last thing they will look for is an attack across el Houl on the port of Akaba. If such a project seems mad even to Auda, how will it seem to the Turks?

AUDA (*chuckling*). There is some wisdom there, el Aurans. They would not even guess at it. No sane man ever would…

LAWRENCE (*taking the map*). But just in case they do, the direction of our march should be northwest at first, to make them believe we are aiming at a raid on the railway.

AUDA (*abstractedly interrupting*). Has Feisal much gold?

LAWRENCE. Alas – he is rich only in promises – and so am I on his behalf.

AUDA. And what would you have promised me if I had consented to this madness?

LAWRENCE. A higher price than the Turks could pay.

AUDA. Then it must be high indeed. What is it?

LAWRENCE. The praise of the whole world for the most brilliant feat of arms in Arabian history.

There is a pause.

AUDA (*gazing at the map*). Akaba! Even your own all-powerful Navy has not dared attack it.

LAWRENCE. Oh yes.

AUDA. And were defeated?

LAWRENCE. Oh no. Our Navy is never defeated.

AUDA. Well?

LAWRENCE. After a successful bombardment they withdrew.

AUDA. Beaten off by the Turkish guns.

LAWRENCE. They are very powerful guns.

AUDA. Have *I* powerful guns?

LAWRENCE. You have no need of guns.

AUDA. How? No need?

LAWRENCE. There is no gun – however powerful – that can fire backwards.

There is a pause.

AUDA. They all point out to sea?

LAWRENCE. All out to sea.

AUDA. Fixed?

LAWRENCE. Fixed.

Another pause.

AUDA. How strong are the Turks?

LAWRENCE. About two thousand in the area.

AUDA. Against five hundred?

LAWRENCE. Four to one. Auda's odds.

AUDA (*chuckling*). Auda's odds. Have they made no preparations against an attack from the land?

LAWRENCE. None.

AUDA. They believe it impossible?

LAWRENCE. A madman's dream.

AUDA (*chuckling*). The fools. What, no fortifications facing the land at all?

LAWRENCE. A few – a very few – but they will be easy to surprise.

AUDA. A camel charge, at night. My battle cry, to panic the idiots from their beds, and then amongst them.

LAWRENCE. They may well surrender at the very sound.

AUDA (*genuinely alarmed*). May Allah forbid! My friend, do you think I am marching across el Houl in the deadliest month of the year, to be rewarded at the end with a tame surrender?

LAWRENCE. Well – then – perhaps no battle cry –

AUDA. That, too, is unthinkable. Even Turks must know who it is that kills them. A charge in daylight, then – after due warning –

LAWRENCE. Not too long a warning.

AUDA. Not too long and not too short Akaba! What a gift to make to Feisal –

LAWRENCE. The gift of Southern Arabia.

The sound of hooves.

CAPTAIN (*off*). Keep the men mounted.

The TURKISH CAPTAIN *walks in, past* LAWRENCE *without glancing at him, halts in front of* AUDA *and salutes.*

God be with you, Auda Abu Tayi!

AUDA. And with you, Captain.

LAWRENCE *moves unobtrusively to go, but finds his escape barred by a* SOLDIER. LAWRENCE *slips to the ground adopting the same squatting attitude in which we first saw him in this scene. He keeps his head lowered. The* CAPTAIN *takes a small box from his pocket.*

CAPTAIN. I bring the greetings and love of my master, the Governor, and the precious gift for which you asked. (*Holds out the box.*)

AUDA (*eagerly snatching it*). By God, but this has been fast work –

CAPTAIN. His Excellency telegraphed to Damascus and had it sent down by the railway.

AUDA. Ah – this is a noble sight. (*Reveals the contents of the package with a delighted flourish. They are a set of false teeth.*) By Allah, these are surely the false teeth of which all other false teeth are but vile and blaspheming copies. Your master's generous answer to his servant's dire need is a great and splendid thing, and will not be forgotten –

CAPTAIN. I shall tell him of your pleasure – it will add to his own.

AUDA. See how they gleam and glitter in the sun. By the prophet, with these in my mouth, I shall be young again. You must eat with me tonight, Captain – and you shall see them in action.

CAPTAIN. I am afraid that will not be possible. I must start back at once.

KERIM *enters from the tent with a pot of coffee. During the ensuing speeches he fills three cups and serves them, first to the* CAPTAIN, *then to* AUDA *and then to* LAWRENCE.

AUDA (*still admiring the teeth*). A pity. You must ask your
   master what gift he would like from me in return –

CAPTAIN. You know the gift.

AUDA. Ah yes, I remember – (*Puts the teeth back in the
   package a trifle abstractedly.*) But tell me, my friend, why
   are you so sure he will come to me?

CAPTAIN. The Governor believes that he'll try to win you to
   the rebel cause.

AUDA. That would be very foolish.

CAPTAIN. Let us hope he is so foolish, Auda. I know my
   master would rather you earned the reward than anyone.

AUDA (*interested*). Reward? You said nothing before of
   a reward.

CAPTAIN. It had not then been authorised.

AUDA (*abstractedly*). How much?

CAPTAIN. Ten thousand pounds.

AUDA (*with a gasp*). Ten thousand! By Allah – is this
   Englishman worth so much?

CAPTAIN. The Governor believes him to be.

AUDA. Ten thousand. (*Suddenly speaking to* LAWRENCE*'s
   lowered head.*) Do you hear that, my friend?

   Pause. LAWRENCE *slowly raises his head.*

LAWRENCE (*looking up at him*). Yes, Auda. I hear it.

AUDA. What do you say?

LAWRENCE. That it is indeed a high price for so low
   a scoundrel.

AUDA. It is a high price. A very high price indeed. Would you
   like to see me win it?

LAWRENCE. I would rather win it, myself. But if not I, then let
   it be you. For surely no reward is too great for Auda Abu Tayi.

   Pause. The CAPTAIN *has glanced at* LAWRENCE *with
   only mild interest.* AUDA *turns back to him.*

AUDA. He speaks loyally and well.

CAPTAIN. He does. (*Reassuringly.*) We have no fears, Auda. We know that you and all the men about you are loyal. But *you* must fear this Englishman. He has a glib and flattering tongue and by it has lured good men into treachery.

AUDA. Below medium height?

CAPTAIN. Yes.

AUDA. And dresses usually in white?

CAPTAIN. So it is said.

AUDA. Looking more English than Arab?

CAPTAIN. Yes. But you won't need to recognise him, Auda. He will surely announce himself to you. And then…

AUDA. And then?

CAPTAIN. You know what to do to gain ten thousand pounds.

AUDA. Yes. I know what to do.

CAPTAIN. I shall give your messages to the Governor.

AUDA (*to* LAWRENCE, *abruptly*). Escort the Captain –

LAWRENCE *rises*.

CAPTAIN. Thank you, but there is no need –

AUDA. Do you think we have no manners here?

CAPTAIN (*smiling*). God be with you, Auda.

AUDA. And with you, Captain.

CAPTAIN (*to* LAWRENCE, *who has stationed himself behind him*). Oh, thank you –

He goes out. AUDA *moves quickly to look after him, looking tense and anxious. We hear the sound of a barked word of command, and of horses' hooves moving away.* AUDA *relaxes and shrugs his shoulders.* LAWRENCE *re-enters.*

AUDA. By heaven, el Aurans, what a joke that was! What a joke to remember –

LAWRENCE (*in a low, uncertain voice*). It won't be easy
    to forget.

AUDA (*touching his arm*). My friend, you are trembling.

LAWRENCE. Yes. I am.

AUDA. You were afraid?

LAWRENCE. Yes.

AUDA. Of what? Of a degenerate Turk and his few followers?
    There are five hundred men in this camp. They could have
    accounted for them in twenty seconds.

LAWRENCE. Yes. They could. The question is whether
    they would.

AUDA. By Allah, they would if I had ordered them.

LAWRENCE. Yes. But would you have ordered them?

AUDA. Can you doubt it?

LAWRENCE. With some ease.

AUDA. But, my friend, if I had wanted the reward…

LAWRENCE. Auda, do you believe your thoughts are so hard
    to read? To betray a guest is a great sin, but ten thousand
    pounds is ten thousand pounds, and surely worth a spin of
    the wheel of fate. If the Turk recognises the foreigner, then
    the foreigner is not betrayed. But, to be recognised, he must
    first be made to raise his head and show the Turk his English
    features and then to stand up to show the Turk his white
    clothes and his meagre height –

AUDA (*chuckling*). What a fool he was, that Turk! (*To*
    LAWRENCE.) Of course I knew he was a fool or I would
    never have taken that risk.

    LAWRENCE *looks at him, without replying*.

Come, my friend. We have plans to make.

    LAWRENCE *makes no move to follow him*.

Very well. I admit that I was tempted. You offered me
    honour and they, money. Both I love exceedingly and not the

one much more than the other. But I spun the wheel and honour won. There is no going back now.

LAWRENCE. And if they raised my price?

AUDA. Ah. But they will not raise your price until after we have taken Akaba.

LAWRENCE *smiles, shrugs his shoulders and goes slowly towards the tent opening.* AUDA *has picked up the package and is looking at his precious false teeth. Suddenly he hurls them to the ground, picks up a rifle and smashes the butt on them, again and again. After a moment he stops, stoops and picks up the shattered fragments, looking at them with eyes of tragic longing. Then he throws them carelessly away.*

The path of honour.

He puts his arm round LAWRENCE *and escorts him into the tent. The lights fade. In the darkness we hear the sound of 'Tipperary' played on a rather scratchy record.*

Scene Eight

Scene: a small hut in a British Army camp near Suez. As the lights come on they focus first on an ancient gramophone, complete with horn. A man is humming the song to this accompaniment and, as the lights come up more strongly, we see he is a BRITISH CORPORAL *and is using a disinfectant spray in time to the music. The camp has been abandoned through an outbreak of plague, and the hut bears a dilapidated appearance. A door is open at the back, showing the night sky.* HAMED, *looking ragged and desert-stained, comes into the hut and looks around.*

CORPORAL (*gesticulating*). *Yellah! Yellah!* Shoo!

HAMED *pays no attention, but walks over to a desk where he has seen a telephone.*

Get out of here, woggie. Go on. Hop it, now – Get out, woggie, or I'll have to shoot you, and you wouldn't like that, now, would you? This is British Army property and I'm in charge – see. Shoo! *Yellah!* Shoo!

HAMED, *still paying no attention to the* CORPORAL*, lifts the receiver rather fearfully to his ear, expecting to be electrocuted. Reassured by his immunity, he listens for a few moments. Still paying no attention to the* CORPORAL *but satisfied, apparently, with what he has heard on the telephone, he replaces the receiver and walks out. The* CORPORAL*, after a shrug, continues his fumigating. The record comes to an end. He is bending over the gramophone as* LAWRENCE *comes in. He looks as travel-stained and dirty as* HAMED.

Cripes! Another one. (*Shouting*). *Yellah! Yellah!* (*Uses his spray on* LAWRENCE.)

LAWRENCE *goes to the telephone.*

Get to hell out of here, woggie! I nearly shot your chum and I'll shoot you, I swear, if you don't buzz off!

LAWRENCE (*at telephone*). Does this telephone work, Corporal?

CORPORAL (*at length*). Did you speak?

LAWRENCE. Yes, I asked if this telephone works. (*Lifts up receiver and listens.*)

CORPORAL (*beyond his depth*). I am in charge of this camp, which is Government property, and which has been closed down on account of plague – and no unauthorised person may...

LAWRENCE (*into telephone*). Naval Headquarters. It's urgent. (*To* CORPORAL.) Ah. Plague. So that explains it. For the last half-hour I've been wondering if the British troops on the Suez Canal had got bored with the war and gone home.

CORPORAL (*pointing to telephone*). Listen – I said no unauthorised person...

LAWRENCE (*into receiver*). Hullo, Naval Headquarters? I want your senior chap, whoever he is... Admiral Makepeace? Right... No. I don't want any duty officer. I want the man in charge... Then get him away from dinner... Then you'll have to forget your orders, won't you?... My name will mean nothing to you and my rank is unimportant, but I can only tell you that if you fail to get your Admiral to the telephone this instant you will probably face a court martial for having delayed the ending of the war by roughly three months... Just hold on a moment... (*Puts his hand over the receiver and turns to the* CORPORAL.) Get me some water from that tap outside, would you, old chap?

CORPORAL. It's not for drinking. Strict orders are to boil all water.

LAWRENCE. The last well I drank from – yesterday morning – had a dead goat in it.

CORPORAL. Yes – er – sir. As you say. (*Goes.*)

LAWRENCE (*into the telephone, mildly*). Now, in answer to your question, I am not off my bleeding chump. I am speaking the simple truth. At your switchboard you hold in your hands the lives of five hundred Allied soldiers and the possession of the most valuable port in Southern Arabia, in which at the moment those soldiers are victoriously sitting, with nothing whatever to eat except their camels or their prisoners, and if I know them, they'll start on the prisoners... Thank you.

The CORPORAL *has come back with a mug of water.* LAWRENCE *takes it from him.*

By jove, Corporal, it's worked. I think he still thinks I'm off my rocker, though.

CORPORAL (*politely*). Does he, sir? Fancy.

LAWRENCE *splutters into the mug from which he is avidly drinking. After a moment he puts it down.*

LAWRENCE. I've got some men outside who need food and drink. Would you look after them?

CORPORAL. Yes, sir. I don't speak their lingo, sir.

LAWRENCE. If you smile at them and treat them as if they were human beings, you'll find them quite easy to handle –

CORPORAL. Yes, sir. I'll do my best. (*Goes out*.)

LAWRENCE (*into telephone*). Oh, hullo, Admiral. Sorry to disturb you… My name's Lawrence, Captain Lawrence… Oh, no. Just Army. Look. I want you to send a destroyer to Akaba… Destroyer, that's right, but it doesn't have to be a destroyer. As a matter of fact a bigger thing might be better. It's got to take a lot of stuff, you see – food for five hundred men, about six howitzers, thirty machine guns, as many grenades and rifles as the Army will let you have, oh, and some armoured cars would come in very handy. Also most important of all really about fifty thousand pounds in cash… Fifty thousand… Oh, I'm sorry. Didn't I tell you… Yes, we took it… From the land. Rather a long way round, but it seemed to work all right… No. They didn't appear to expect us… Oh, about five hundred killed and seven hundred prisoners… Ours? Two. Unhappily we lost five more on the march, including one of my bodyguards. You see conditions in the desert were a bit – rough. We had three bad sandstorms, and I'm afraid my compass work wasn't all that good, and we missed a well – … No, Admiral, I promise you this isn't a joke. Akaba is ours… A rather picturesque fellow called Auda Abu Tayi is holding it, but don't let him sell it to you, because he'll certainly try. Now you will get that boat there tonight, won't you? You see, the Turks are bound to react violently, and mount a counteroffensive in the next few days. Will you please inform Cairo for me? I'm a bit tired… No, I won't be available tomorrow. I shall be asleep tomorrow and probably the next day. If they want to talk to me after that they'll find me in my old office in Cairo… Making maps… Yes. The C-in-C does know of me. In fact, General Murray and I have often exchanged words… Gone? Gone for good? (*Plainly delighted*.) Oh dear! Who, then… Allenby? No. I've not heard of him. Thank you, sir. Goodnight. (*Rings off and rests his head on the desk*.)

HAMED *stalks angrily into the office, holding a tin of corned beef, keeping it as far away from him as possible.* LAWRENCE *looks up*.

What is it, Hamed?

HAMED *thrusts the tin angrily at him.* LAWRENCE *takes it.*

Ah, I see. The infidel Corporal has not understood the laws of Allah. You must forgive him. (*Puts the tin on the floor.*) Since Rashid died I have not seen you smile, Hamed. Not once. But before you had begun to learn the trick. (*Quietly.*) Tell me. Is it that you blame me?

HAMED *signifies dissent.*

You can tell me if it is true. I shall understand.

HAMED *again signifies dissent.*

You smile, then, at no one? At nothing?

HAMED *signifies agreement.*

Because of your grief, and only because of that?

HAMED *signifies assent.*

I am sorry, Hamed. I will not insult you by trying to tell you that one day you will forget. I know as well as you that you will not. But, at least, in time you will not remember as fiercely as you do now – and I pray that that time may be soon. I shall see that the Corporal gives you food more fitting to Moslem warriors. I want anyway to say goodbye to you all. (*Rises, showing his utter exhaustion. His back is turned to us as* HAMED *speaks.*)

HAMED (*with certainty*). You will come back to us, el Aurans.

LAWRENCE *turns slowly to look at him. There is a long pause.*

LAWRENCE. Others will come, Hamed. Many others of my countrymen. That is certain.

HAMED. There are no others we need, but you.

There is a pause. The telephone rings. LAWRENCE *makes no move to pick up the receiver.*

You must come back to us, el Aurans. It is you that we need.

LAWRENCE (*finally picking up receiver*). Yes… Yes, this is Lawrence… Who? Flag Lieutenant? Hold on a moment.

(*Covers the receiver.*) Go to the men, Hamed. I'll join you there.

HAMED *turns to go.*

And, Hamed –

HAMED *turns.*

Thank you for your words. Any words from you would have been welcome, but those words more welcome than all.

HAMED *goes.*

(*Into receiver.*) I'm sorry… To get across the Canal? Well, I thought I'd get some fellow to row me… The Admiral's barge? I say, how splendid. Thank you. (*Rings off. Softly.*) Ross, are you still dreaming of me? Can you hear me? Ross? (*Pause.*) I've done it. Done it. I've captured Akaba. I've done what no professional soldier would have dared to do. I've captured the key to Southern Arabia with five hundred inefficient, untrustworthy Arab bandits. Why don't you enjoy the memory? What makes you so unhappy? Is it that Moroccan I shot in the desert and couldn't kill cleanly because my hand was shaking so? The mangled Turkish bodies in the dynamited trains? Those men who died in the desert?… Rashid?… Is it Rashid? (*Pause.*) War is war, after all. The enemy has to be killed and our own men have to die. And surely, at least I've been more sparing of them than any red-tabbed superman? (*Pause. Angrily.*) What is wrong in trying to write my name in history? Lawrence of Akaba – perhaps – who knows? (*Pause.*) Oh, Ross – how did I become you?

Curtain.

ACT TWO

Scene One

Scene: ALLENBY*'s room in GHQ, Cairo. There is an imposing desk, a large wall map, and comfortable armchairs; behind the desk sits* ALLENBY.

A very decorative ADC *steps smartly into the room and comes to parade-ground attention.*

ADC. Excuse me, sir.

ALLENBY. Are they here?

ADC. Yes, sir.

ALLENBY. Show them in.

> *The* ADC *exits. After a moment the* ADC *re-enters and stands to one side.* STORRS *and* BARRINGTON *enter.*

> Good morning, Colonel. Ah, Storrs – good of you to come.

> *The* ADC *exits.*

STORRS. Not at all, sir. Even in my lax office a request from the Commander-in-Chief is usually counted as an order.

ALLENBY (*not smiling*). Sit down, gentlemen, please.

> *They do so.*

> I've called you here because I understand you both know this fellow Lawrence.

> *They signify assent.*

> I don't want to hear too much of what you think of him as a man. I'm prepared to form my own judgement on that. I'm seeing him later on. I want you to tell me what you think of him as a potential leader. Storrs?

STORRS. Lawrence as a leader? (*Thoughtfully.*) He's pure intellectual, and not by nature a man of action at all. He's strongly introverted, withdrawn and self-conscious, and will never allow anyone to see his true nature. He hides everything behind a manner that's either over-meek, over-arrogant, or over-flippant, whichever is going to disconcert the most. He thinks far too much for the good of his soul and feels far too much for the good of his mind. Consequently he's a highly unstable personality. Finally, he has a sublime contempt for authority – in any form, but chiefly military.

ALLENBY. I see. Not very promising –

STORRS. On the contrary, sir. I think he'd make a military leader of the highest class.

ALLENBY (*snapping*). Why?

STORRS. Because I find to my surprise that I've just given a description of most great commanders from Julius Caesar to Napoleon.

ALLENBY (*nodding after a moment*). Barrington?

BARRINGTON. I disagree, sir, I'm afraid. I don't deny his success in Akaba – though how much luck there was in that, we'll never know. (*Angrily.*) But give him all credit for Akaba – it still makes no difference. He's irresponsible – a useful man, no doubt, to have charging around behind the enemy lines with his Bedouins blowing up trains. But in a position of responsibility – no. Definitely, no. May I ask, sir, what appointment you had in mind?

ALLENBY. In a report to me he has recommended a plan for general revolt of all the Arab peoples in the north – to be timed to coincide with my offensive through the Gaza Gap in November. (*To* BARRINGTON.) By the way, security must be dangerously bad here for him to have known both the time and the place of my offensive.

BARRINGTON *and* STORRS *register discomfort.*

BARRINGTON. On the contrary, sir, security here is very good. I didn't know either time or place and I'm sure Storrs didn't – did you?

STORRS. No.

ALLENBY. Well, then, how on earth did *he*?

BARRINGTON. Guesswork.

STORRS. One of the qualities of a leader, isn't it?

ALLENBY. Possibly. Still, I wish he'd confine his attention to the enemy's plans, and not to mine. However, he suggests that, to support my offensive, four separate Arab forces should be organised to operate east of the Hejaz Railway, between Maan and Damascus here – (*Points*.) along the Turks' main line of communication.

A pause.

BARRINGTON (*ironically*). A rather ambitious plan, isn't it?

ALLENBY (*shortly*). Highly, but I'm accepting it. In fact, I'm accepting all his recommendations, except one – that a high-ranking officer he appointed to direct these operations. I'm thinking of appointing Lawrence himself.

BARRINGTON (*pained*). A captain?

ALLENBY. He was gazetted major this morning. And I've recommended him for an award.

BARRINGTON. I'm afraid my opinion must remain that it would be a very dangerous appointment. Forgive my frankness, sir.

ALLENBY (*dryly*). It does you credit. Storrs?

STORRS. I'll stick to my opinion too.

ALLENBY (*presses a bell on his desk*). I'm grateful to you both.

The ADC *appears.*

Is Major Lawrence here?

ADC. He's just arrived, sir.

ALLENBY. Send him in.

ADC. Yes, sir. (*Salutes and exits.*)

ALLENBY (*to* STORRS). I'm a bit scared of this meeting. Do you think he'll try to floor me with Baudelaire or something?

STORRS. Very likely, sir.

ALLENBY. I wonder if I could floor him with my pet subject.

BARRINGTON. What's that, sir?

ALLENBY. Flowers.

BARRINGTON looks startled. A door is opened and LAWRENCE comes in. He is dressed in a uniform that was never from Savile Row, but now – after loss of weight in the desert – hardly fits him at all. He sees STORRS first.

LAWRENCE. Oh, hullo, Storrs. I was coming to see you this aft–

A firm sign from STORRS indicates the Commander-in-Chief.

Oh, I'm sorry.

He delivers a rather informal-looking salute. Even ALLENBY, determined to be surprised at nothing, has to comment.

ALLENBY. Good gracious!

LAWRENCE. What's the matter?

ALLENBY. Do you always salute like that?

LAWRENCE. Why, sir? Is it wrong?

ALLENBY. It's a little – individual.

LAWRENCE. I was never taught.

ALLENBY. But you must have done some drill training, surely?

LAWRENCE. Well, no. I was a civilian in the Map Section of the War Office in 1914 and one of my jobs was to take maps along to some old General – and he always used to roar at me that he hated civilians in his office and why the dickens wasn't I in uniform? So, one day, I went out to the Army and Navy Stores and bought one.

ALLENBY (*unsmiling*). Do you mean that you've never been given a commission?

LAWRENCE. I don't think so, sir. No, I'm sure I'd remember it if I had.

ALLENBY. I see. Well, I'm happy to inform you that you've now been gazetted a major.

LAWRENCE (*mildly*). Oh? Good.

ALLENBY. And I've recommended you for the CB.

LAWRENCE (*startled*). CB?

ALLENBY. Companion of the Bath.

LAWRENCE. Oh. Thank you.

ALLENBY (*to the other two*). Very well, gentlemen. Thank you very much.

They turn to go.

LAWRENCE. Oh, Storrs. (*To* ALLENBY.) Excuse me.

ALLENBY *nods.*

Freddie Strong has dug up something at Luxor which I know you'll go absolutely mad about.

STORRS, *detained at the door, is looking acutely embarrassed.* BARRINGTON *flashes* ALLENBY *his parade-ground salute and exits.*

(*Apparently oblivious.*) It's a small alabaster perfume jar, exquisite shape, twentieth dynasty I should think, with what seems like a strong Minoan influence –

ALLENBY (*quietly*). Minoan influence in the twentieth dynasty?

LAWRENCE *turns to look at him, apparently seeing him for the first time.*

LAWRENCE (*at length*). I suppose it couldn't be, could it? I must have got the dynasty wrong.

ALLENBY. Or the influence,

LAWRENCE (*slowly*). Yes. Or the influence.

ALLENBY (*with authority*). Goodbye, Storrs, and thank you.

STORRS. Goodbye, sir.

He goes with evident relief.

ALLENBY. Sit down, Lawrence.

LAWRENCE *sits. There is a pause.*

(*Smiling suddenly.*) Tell me – did Freddie Strong really dig up a twentieth-dynasty perfume jar?

There is a pause while LAWRENCE *and* ALLENBY *look at each other appraisingly across the large desk.*

LAWRENCE (*with a good-humoured shrug*). Well, he does dig things up all the time, you know.

ALLENBY (*nodding appreciatively*). Good. I'm glad we understand each other so soon.

LAWRENCE (*without rancour*). Yes. So am I.

ALLENBY. I was lucky with the Minoan influence. I've just been reading Arthur Evans' book, *The Palace of Minos in Crete.*

LAWRENCE (*politely*). It's pleasant to meet a General who's read anything except Clausewitz.

ALLENBY. Yes. You won't catch me on Clausewitz, although I confess I'm a bit rusty. But please don't try me on the campaigns of Belisarius. I gather that *is* one of your pet subjects?

LAWRENCE. Yes. How did you know?

ALLENBY. I've made it my business to find out. No doubt you've done the same about me.

LAWRENCE. Flowers?

ALLENBY. Correct.

LAWRENCE. Shakespeare, Chippendale, mobile warfare, Chopin and children. Not, of course, necessarily, in that order.

ALLENBY. Your spies have done even better than mine.

LAWRENCE. I expect yours had less to find out.

ALLENBY. More, I think – but your talent for self-concealment is greater.

LAWRENCE. Perhaps it needs to be.

ALLENBY. Perhaps.

LAWRENCE (*smiling*). A lesser man would have said: 'Oh no
– I'm sure not.'

ALLENBY. I'm not interested in the secrets of your soul,
Lawrence. I'm interested in only one thing. Are you the right
man for the job?

LAWRENCE (*genuinely puzzled*). What job?

ALLENBY (*impatiently holding up* LAWRENCE*'s report and
tapping it*). This, of course.

LAWRENCE (*still puzzled*). My report? (*Gets up, evidently
really disturbed.*) Oh no. Great heavens, no. Not me. That
would be disastrous. (*Plainly agitated.*)

ALLENBY *looks at him enquiringly, evidently wondering
whether this is not just another trick.*

ALLENBY. You echo Colonel Barrington.

LAWRENCE. Even Colonel Barrington can be right once in
a war's duration. He is now.

ALLENBY. You surprise me.

LAWRENCE. Why?

ALLENBY. I thought you were an ambitious man.

LAWRENCE. So I am.

ALLENBY. Well, here might be your chance.

LAWRENCE (*shaking his head*). I've had my chance. Akaba
and being made a Major, and the – what's the thing – CB –
that's enough, isn't it?

ALLENBY (*thoughtfully*). I wouldn't have thought so – for
you. When you were writing this report, did it never occur to
you I might consider you for the job?

LAWRENCE. Of course it did. That's why I was so determined
to make it plain exactly what qualities your man would need.
He must be a man of authority, with the patience to remain
cheerful in the face of incompetence, cowardice, greed and

treachery. He must have a deep practical knowledge of strategy, and of the principles of irregular warfare. Above all he must know how to lie and flatter and cheat in a cause that is not his own, but in which he must appear to believe. And he must forget that he's ever heard of the Sykes-Picot Agreement.

ALLENBY. What agreement?

LAWRENCE (*impatiently*). The secret treaty partitioning post-war Arabia between the French and us.

ALLENBY. I've never heard of it

LAWRENCE. No? Nor, for the moment, has Feisal, but if he finds out there'll be hell to pay. So it's vital that he and his people should continually be fed, from now on, the right kind of lies by the right kind of liar. Therefore this man of yours has to be a very senior officer. Then his lies will have real weight.

ALLENBY. I thought you didn't approve of senior officers.

LAWRENCE. I don't approve of the man I've just described. And nor, I suspect, do you. But it's the man you want for the job. Not me, General.

ALLENBY. Possibly. The difficulty is that another man hasn't already operated successfully for months behind the Turkish lines, hasn't already won the trust of the Arab rebels, and hasn't taken Akaba.

LAWRENCE. What does Akaba prove?

ALLENBY. Enough.

LAWRENCE. Do you know why I took Akaba? Do you know why I went off alone into the desert in the first place?

ALLENBY. Escape from an office?

LAWRENCE. A little true.

ALLENBY. Escape from yourself?

LAWRENCE. I'm a Greek scholar. I have a profound belief in the virtues of self-knowledge.

ALLENBY. A man can have a belief without practising it.

LAWRENCE (*appreciatively*). I grant you the point. Escape from myself then. What else?

ALLENBY. Escape from too much thinking?

LAWRENCE. No. You can't escape from that, even in the desert.

ALLENBY. But the desert is a cleaner place to think in than an office.

LAWRENCE. There's nothing clean or dirty but thinking makes it so. And death is dirty, even in the desert. Still, I grant you the point.

ALLENBY. Finally, a burning desire to show off to my predecessor, General Murray?

LAWRENCE. Also true. (*Admiringly.*) I must say you've done pretty well, so far.

ALLENBY. Thank you. (*Politely.*) Well, now, shall we get back to the business on hand?

LAWRENCE (*sadly*). This *is* the business on hand, I'm afraid. You've diagnosed my motives for Akaba and the rest of it quite accurately although you left out the most important one of all – a cold-blooded experiment with willpower – but at least you must admit that all these motives have one thing in common. They're all flagrantly selfish.

ALLENBY. Possibly. Does that matter?

LAWRENCE. This job is for a Messiah. For a visionary with real faith – not for an intellectual misfit.

ALLENBY (*offhandedly*). But you like the Arabs, don't you?

LAWRENCE. It's not enough to like them. Your man must believe in them and their destiny.

ALLENBY. What about your own country and *its* destiny?

LAWRENCE (*quietly*). Oh yes. I believe in that. And I grant you that in war my country has a perfect right to demand my life. I doubt if it has the right to demand more.

ALLENBY. Aren't you exaggerating the demands of this job a bit?

LAWRENCE (*simply*). No. You're a trained commander, you see. When you send men out to die, you don't question whether it's *right* – only whether it's *wise*. If it's unwise, it's wrong, and only then your conscience pricks. My conscience isn't Sandhurst-trained. It's as undrilled as my salute, and so soft it must have the armour-plating of a cause to believe in. (*After a pause*.) How on earth can one *think* oneself into a belief?

There is a pause.

ALLENBY (*again offhandedly*). I suppose one can't. But mightn't it be possible to will oneself into it?

A pause.

LAWRENCE (*laughing*). You're a bit of a Mephisto, aren't you?

ALLENBY. I'm flattered to be thought so.

LAWRENCE. Do you know, General – I think you and I might get along very well.

ALLENBY. I'm sure I hope so, Major.

Pause.

LAWRENCE. Well, the first thing will be money.

ALLENBY. How much?

LAWRENCE. The Turks are lavish spenders and we shall have to outbid them. Say two hundred thousand.

ALLENBY (*doubtfully*). Hm.

LAWRENCE (*cheerfully*). Thinking of the Treasury? Put it under the head of propaganda. They'll like that. It's fashionable. I shall want it all in gold, of course. The Arabs distrust bits of paper. (*Turning to the map*.) Akaba must be made the main Arab base, instead of Jeddah; and I suggest you put Colonel Joyce in charge of it.

ALLENBY. What about Colonel Barrington?

LAWRENCE. Oh, put him on somebody's staff. Make him a General, I'm sure he's overdue. Now the most important thing of all, and this you *must* do –

ALLENBY (*mildly*). One moment, Major Lawrence. I think I must remind you that I have not yet offered you this appointment.

LAWRENCE. No. Nor you have. And I haven't accepted it yet either. Still, I might as well give you my views – don't you think – as I'm here. So – proceeding – Feisal must be detached from the forces of the Sherif of Mecca and made Commander-in-Chief of all Arab forces in the field, under the orders of yourself. And – for reasons purely of prestige – a small regular Arab force must be formed and trained to operate frontally at the decisive moment – but, of course, our main and vital effort will continue to lie in irregular operations behind the enemy lines. (*After a moment.*) I think that's all.

ALLENBY. Good.

LAWRENCE. Well. I'd better not take up any more of your time, General. I'm sure you've got a host of important things to do. So I'll be off now, if that's all right.

ALLENBY. That's all right.

LAWRENCE. I've got a few things to turn over in my mind, too. By the way, some time you must convert me about Chippendale. I've always thought he was overrated. But I'm rather a Philistine about furniture. I don't use it much, you see. (*At the door.*) Well, goodbye, sir.

ALLENBY. Goodbye.

LAWRENCE. And I suppose I shall hear from you?

ALLENBY. Yes. You'll hear from me.

> LAWRENCE *flashes a smile of farewell, turns to the door, and then turns back, having evidently forgotten something. He produces his eccentric salute.*

> One of these days I really must show you how to do that.

LAWRENCE. Yes, sir, when we both have the time. (*Exits.*)

Scene Two

An ornate room with two exits. When the lights come up, the
TURKISH GENERAL *reclining on a divan. He is speaking into*
the mouthpiece of a Dictaphone. The TURKISH CAPTAIN *is*
sitting carelessly on a chair looking at a magazine of nudes.
The ORDERLY *and* TURKISH SOLDIER *are standing at the*
entrances.

GENERAL. Circular telegram to all centres of Turkish Military
Intelligence, Central Arabia. Most secret. Begins. Despite all
our endeavours and the raising of the reward for Lawrence's
capture to the unprecedented sum of twenty thousand
pounds, he remains at large, operating behind our lines. The
elimination of this terrorist has now become of vital concern,
not only to the success of our military operations, but to the
very continuance of our dominion in Arabia.

CAPTAIN. You're making him sound too important. You don't
want to start a panic, do you?

GENERAL (*mildly*). Don't interrupt. Read your magazine. (*Into
the Dictaphone.*) Since his return to Arabia six months ago
Lawrence has been known to have contacted secret
revolutionary groups in places as far apart as Jerusalem,
Damascus and Beirut. At present he is reported to be
operating in the district of Deraa itself. His aim is, probably,
to start a general uprising against us, timed to coincide with
a British offensive in Palestine. Meanwhile he continues his
guerrilla activities against our lines of communication. All
this poses a threat that must on no account be taken lightly.

CAPTAIN (*angrily*). Can you see them taking it lightly? They
already think he has supernatural powers.

GENERAL (*into the Dictaphone*). Paragraph two. Certain
additional facts on Lawrence have now come to light. One.
Despite rumours to the contrary he does not wear female
disguise. The recent practice of forcible unveiling of women
will therefore cease. Two. The description of Lawrence as
already circulated is accurate and has been vouched for –
(*With a look at the* CAPTAIN.) by an officer of my staff,
who once came into close contact with him.

CAPTAIN (*jumping up*). Delete that.

GENERAL (*mildly*). I wasn't going to say which member of my staff.

CAPTAIN. You would if Constantinople asked.

GENERAL. I will – if you don't sit down and keep quiet. (*Into the Dictaphone.*) Three. In view of information recently come to hand regarding Lawrence's sexual proclivities, the watch at present being maintained on brothels and similar places may be discontinued –

CAPTAIN (*eagerly*). O-oh! That's interesting. What information?

GENERAL. I'm sorry to disappoint you. The information was decisively negative.

CAPTAIN. In every way?

GENERAL. Yes.

CAPTAIN. That doesn't seem likely to me.

GENERAL (*genially*). I'm sure it doesn't, but ascetics do exist, you know.

CAPTAIN. But no one is born an ascetic. Is Lawrence very religious?

GENERAL. His self-denial is self-imposed. It has also a very revealing aspect.

CAPTAIN. What?

GENERAL. He avoids physical contact of any kind. Even shaking hands requires an effort.

CAPTAIN. I don't see what's so revealing about that –

GENERAL. Don't you. (*Into the Dictaphone.*) Paragraph four –

CAPTAIN (*sulkily*). What does it reveal?

GENERAL (*patiently*). A rebellious body, a strong will and a troubled spirit. May I go on?

CAPTAIN. You mean he'd like to, but won't admit he'd like to, and so he doesn't?

GENERAL. You put it very subtly. (*Into the Dictaphone.*) Paragraph four. Most important. It must be brought to the attention of all personnel that the capture of Lawrence alive should now be their primary objective. When captured the criminal will not be interrogated locally, but will be handed over forthwith to the requisite high authority. By Order Military Governor, District of Deraa. Message ends.

He puts down the mouthpiece and gestures to the ORDERLY. *The* ORDERLY *pours a glass of wine and hands it to the* GENERAL.

A real French Burgundy. (*Drinks.*) Have some?

The CAPTAIN *shakes his head disapprovingly.*

You're such a good boy. (*Examining the glass.*) I'm so glad I'm not a Christian. In their religion this isn't a sin –

CAPTAIN. If I capture Lawrence, I shall shoot the swine.

GENERAL (*mildly*). You really are very foolish, aren't you. Your bullet might well lose us Arabia. Can't you see that the man's death, by itself, would solve nothing? The Arabs would go on believing in this myth that he's taught them, Arabia for the Arabs – one race, one land, one nation. For a thousand years out here before he came, that idea was only the harmless dream of a few religious fanatics. But he's shown them the way to turn it into fact. Only half a fact as yet, Allah be praised, but even that half is a grave danger to our Empire. The whole fact? Well, then the world is in danger.

CAPTAIN (*carelessly*). The world can sleep easily, I think.

GENERAL (*gravely*). Feisal has chosen Damascus as his capital.

The CAPTAIN *laughs.*

I'd laugh too if I didn't know that the brain that planted that fantasy is as brilliant, ice-cold and ruthless as any revolutionary's in history. Do you really think that a bullet in that brain will turn the Arabs back now?

CAPTAIN (*shrugging*). What will?

Pause. The GENERAL *sips his wine.*

GENERAL. Well, I suppose that what a brain can create, the same brain can destroy.

CAPTAIN. Get him to recant, you mean?

GENERAL. It's the traditional method of dealing with heresy.

CAPTAIN. But how do you do it?

GENERAL (*shrugging*). By persuasion, I suppose. (*Looking at him.*) What a pity about this climate. It ruins a fair complexion. It shouldn't have affected yours, though, with your Circassian blood.

CAPTAIN. I have no Circassian blood.

GENERAL. I thought you told me that you had.

CAPTAIN. It was you who told me that I had.

GENERAL. Some time ago, I imagine.

CAPTAIN. I don't think you'll get Lawrence to recant by torture.

GENERAL. Who said anything about torture? Persuasion was the word I used.

CAPTAIN (*incredulously*). You'd argue him into it?

GENERAL. Isn't that the best way of getting someone to admit he's wrong? After all, he is wrong. The Arabs' readiness for statehood is a lie and he knows it. That should give his interrogator a considerable advantage. To get him to admit that it's a lie? Difficult. With a man of faith, a real fanatic – like Feisal – impossible. But with an intellectual Englishman who believes only in his own will – and who avoids shaking hands… One would probably have to start by teaching him a few of the facts of life.

CAPTAIN. Surely if he's an intellectual he must know the facts of life.

The GENERAL *laughs.*

Have I said something stupid?

GENERAL. Don't let it concern you. (*Empties his glass.*) Yes, it's a strange relationship I have with Lawrence. He doesn't even know of my existence, while I probably already know more about him than he knows about himself. I wish all relationships were so pleasant and uncomplicated.

He looks at the CAPTAIN, *who looks away.*

There's one thing I don't know about him. I wonder if he really believes that all the sacrifice is worth it.

The ORDERLY *has refilled his glass.*

CAPTAIN. Sacrifice? Sacrifice of what?

GENERAL (*taking a sip of his wine and ruffling the* CAPTAIN'*s hair*). Oh, of everything that makes life worth living.

The lights fade.

Scene Three

Scene: a railway embankment. Reclining against a rock is LAWRENCE, *dressed in inconspicuously ragged Arab clothes and scratching a plan on a piece of slate.* HAMED *comes on, carrying a small box which he puts on the ground and sits beside it. There is a silence as* LAWRENCE *continues to sketch.* HAMED *feels in his clothes for a chicken bone, which he proceeds to gnaw.*

HAMED (*at length*). Bad news. (*Indicates box.*) They refused the money, and promised nothing.

LAWRENCE (*still sketching*). Why?

HAMED (*between bites*). Frightened. With good cause. Of the three men you visited in this town last month, two have been arrested and the other is in hiding. But they have his family and the families of the other two.

LAWRENCE (*after a pause*). Who talked?

HAMED. One of Dakhil's children. It seems you gave him
a present – an English halfpenny. He showed it in the market
and tried to sell it. The great el Aurans had given it to him,
he said. A policeman heard him.

A pause.

LAWRENCE. Is Dakhil arrested?

HAMED. Yes, and Ali. It was Suleiman who escaped.

LAWRENCE (*still sketching*). But they have his family?

HAMED. Yes. Even the old grandmother. Or so they say.

A pause.

LAWRENCE. An English halfpenny. It was there with the gold.
I don't know why. Because it was bigger and brighter the
child wanted it and I let him play with it. I meant to get it
back from him when I left – but – I forgot. (*With sudden
tension in his voice.*) I forgot. (*Resumes his sketching. In
a level voice.*) Have they killed Dakhil and Ali?

HAMED (*shrugging*). Let us hope so.

LAWRENCE. Yes.

HAMED. What are you doing?

LAWRENCE. Drawing a plan of the Deraa airfield. Also that
road, down there in the valley, along which our men will
march – when the day comes.

HAMED. Will the day come?

LAWRENCE (*gently*). You only ask that to anger me, Hamed.
It pleases you sometimes to anger me. You know the day
will come.

HAMED. But when?

LAWRENCE (*after a pause*). In Allah and Allenby's good time.

HAMED. Sometimes I think both have deserted us.

LAWRENCE. They haven't – but if you talk like that, they may.
And so may I.

HAMED. You? (*The thought is plainly laughable to* HAMED. *He stretches himself out, and belches happily.*) What will happen after we win the war? Will you make Prince Feisal King of all Arabia?

LAWRENCE. It won't be for me to make anybody king of anything, Hamed. Prince Feisal will choose for himself. Who am I to make kings?

HAMED (*after a pause*). There was a story in our camp at Azrak last night that the English King and the French President have made an agreement after the war to divide Arabia between them. The English will take all the lands beyond the Jordan and the French will take Syria and the north.

A pause.

LAWRENCE (*with bland unconcern*). You have a fine ear for a story, Hamed.

HAMED. The Headman of Russia – a great and noble rebel – whose name I don't remember…

LAWRENCE. Lenin.

HAMED. Yes, Lenin. He has told it to the world. It was an agreement made two years ago – before you came to us, el Aurans –

LAWRENCE (*interrupting*). The great and noble rebel lies in his teeth. There is no such agreement. Could there be, and I not know?

HAMED (*after a pause*). You could be lying to us. You could have lied to us from the beginning.

He has said it for fun, hoping to get an irritated response from LAWRENCE. LAWRENCE, *however, does not answer nor meet his glance.*

(*Rather pathetically, after a pause.*) That was a joke, el Aurans.

LAWRENCE. Yes, Hamed, I know. (*Continues his sketch.*) Whenever you hear this story again, will you remember that you are my friend, and beat the man who tells it?

HAMED. Yes. (*Without moving.*) There are two Turkish soldiers walking towards us.

LAWRENCE (*also not moving*). Did they see me sketching?

HAMED. I don't know.

LAWRENCE. Have you anything on you, if you are searched?

HAMED. The gold and the list.

LAWRENCE. Be asleep. We don't know each other. Whatever happens, have nothing to do with me.

> HAMED *obediently closes his eyes.* LAWRENCE *placidly continues to sketch as a* TURKISH SERGEANT *and the* TURKISH SOLDIER *come on, apparently not noticing them. Then they stop and the* SERGEANT *walks back to* LAWRENCE.

SERGEANT. An artist?

LAWRENCE. I get pleasure in this, but I am no artist.

SERGEANT. Let me see.

LAWRENCE. I would not affront your Excellency's eyes. (*Drops the sketch on to his lap.*)

SERGEANT. You have a white skin for these parts. What is your race?

LAWRENCE. Circassian.

SERGEANT. Circassian? They are rare here.

LAWRENCE. Yes. We are rare.

SERGEANT. What are you doing in Deraa?

LAWRENCE. My business is lawful.

SERGEANT. What is it?

LAWRENCE. Travelling.

SERGEANT. Where to?

LAWRENCE. Damascus.

SERGEANT. On your feet, Circassian.

LAWRENCE *gets up quietly, apparently not alarmed.*

You're lying, aren't you?

LAWRENCE. Why should I lie to your Excellency?

SERGEANT. I think you're a deserter.

LAWRENCE. With respect, we Circassians are exempt from
military service –

SERGEANT. Don't argue. You're of military age, and therefore
a deserter.

LAWRENCE. The argument has force, but hardly logic. By
a special decree...

SERGEANT (*smiling*). You want logic, do you?

He draws his revolver. The SOLDIER *cocks his rifle.*

Well, here it is. (*Pokes* LAURENCE *in the side with the
revolver. Quite mildly.*) Now come with me.

LAWRENCE. Where to?

SERGEANT. Why should I tell you?

He digs him in the ribs. LAWRENCE *drops the sketch, then
stoops to pick it up. He glances at it. Then carelessly
crumples it up and throws it away. It lands close to* HAMED.
He goes off with the SERGEANT *and the* SOLDIER.
HAMED, *as if in sleep, puts an arm out and picks up the
drawing. The lights fade.*

Scene Four

Scene: the lights came on slowly to reveal the TURKISH
GENERAL *sitting in his room in an attitude and with an
expression that denotes considerable nervous tension. He
seems, too, to be straining to hear something, but it is not
apparent what; although, at one moment, we hear a shout of
harsh laughter, cut off abruptly by the evident closing of a door.
The* CAPTAIN *comes in rapidly.*

CAPTAIN. What in the name of God is going on in the
guardroom?

There is a pause.

GENERAL. They're beating a deserter.

CAPTAIN. Your orders?

GENERAL. Yes.

CAPTAIN. Why?

GENERAL (*after a pause*). He was insolent.

CAPTAIN. I didn't see much. I don't like those sights. But I did
see a white skin. At least it *was* white, I suppose?

GENERAL. Yes.

CAPTAIN. A Circassian?

GENERAL. Yes.

CAPTAIN. Do I guess accurately at the form his insolence took?

GENERAL. I expect so.

A pause.

CAPTAIN. If it's reported there could be trouble.

GENERAL. I don't think so.

CAPTAIN. You should put a stop to it.

GENERAL. Why?

CAPTAIN. They look as if they might kill him.

GENERAL. He can stop it himself. He can stop it at any second. He has only to say 'yes'.

A pause.

CAPTAIN. By the look I caught of him he's not paying you much of a compliment.

GENERAL. No.

CAPTAIN. I'm going to stop it.

GENERAL. No.

CAPTAIN. I'm going to. For your sake, as much as his.

He goes to the door. The GENERAL *moves swiftly towards him and grips him.*

GENERAL (*quietly*). Now, listen carefully. It will be better for you if you don't go down there.

The CAPTAIN, *struggles free and exits. The* GENERAL *turns back into the room. The* CAPTAIN *comes back, and stares at him with unbelieving eyes.*

CAPTAIN (*violently*). Do you know who it is? (*Reads his answer in the* GENERAL*'s face*). So that's why you tried to stop me from going down there.

GENERAL. I told you it would be better for you if you didn't.

CAPTAIN. Is that a threat?

GENERAL. Yes. Did you say anything to the men?

CAPTAIN. No.

GENERAL (*strength returning to his voice*). You will say nothing to anyone, now or at any time. If you do, I'll have you shot. He's a Circassian deserter, called Mohammed Ibn Dheilan. He comes from Kuneitra. He is being punished for insolence.

CAPTAIN (*with disgust*). Punished? Do you know what they're doing to him now?

GENERAL. They've stopped beating him?

CAPTAIN. Yes.

GENERAL. I see.

CAPTAIN (*hysterically*). What they're doing to him now – are those your orders too?

There is no reply from the GENERAL.

I thought you couldn't have known – not even you, I thought, could have ordered that.

GENERAL. You misjudged me.

CAPTAIN. I hate the man, but this is vile and horrible.

GENERAL. It's vile and horrible to be mangled in a wrecked troop train.

CAPTAIN. So it's revenge.

GENERAL. No. If it were I might enjoy it.

CAPTAIN. What about your talk that you'd persuade him to admit he's been wrong?

GENERAL. What about it?

CAPTAIN. Is this what you meant?

GENERAL. I said, if you remember, that his interrogator might have to start by teaching him a few of the facts of life.

CAPTAIN. And this is only the beginning?

GENERAL. It may be the ending too.

CAPTAIN (*muttering*). You mean he may die under it?

GENERAL. No. They have my orders not to kill him. I mean that if this succeeds tonight it will be the end for him. Body violated, will broken, enemy destroyed. (*Sharply.*) There's someone on the stairs.

CAPTAIN. They're bringing him up. (*Hysterically.*) I don't want to see it.

GENERAL. Control yourself.

The TURKISH SERGEANT *and the* TURKISH SOLDIER *appear on the threshold. They are supporting* LAWRENCE *between them. He is half-conscious and his head has fallen onto his chest.*

(*Quietly.*) Very well, Captain. Report to me in the morning.

The CAPTAIN *comes automatically to attention. Then he goes out, averting his eyes from the sight of* LAWRENCE *as he passes him.*

(*To* SERGEANT.) Well?

The SERGEANT, *with a broad grin, nods slowly.*

He said yes?

The SERGEANT *shakes his head, still grinning. The* GENERAL *looks at him questioningly.*

SERGEANT (*at length*). He didn't need to say it.

The GENERAL, *after a pause, nods quietly.*

He's a strange one, this, General, I'm telling you.

GENERAL (*sharply*). All right. Let him go.

The two men release LAWRENCE *whose knees buckle under him. He slips face downwards and motionless on to the floor.*

Get out.

The two men go. The GENERAL *goes slowly over to* LAWRENCE. *He kneels down and, quite gently, pulls his head back and looks at him.*

(*Quietly.*) You must understand that I know. (*Replaces* LAWRENCE*'s head gently on the floor.*) You can hear me, I think. (*Slowly repeating.*) You must understand that I know.

There is no sign from LAWRENCE *that he has heard. Throughout the ensuing scene he remains completely motionless.*

I do pity you, you know. You won't ever believe it, but it's true. I know what was revealed to you tonight, and I know what that revelation will have done to you. You can think I mean just a broken will, if you like. That might have destroyed you by itself. But I mean more than that. Far more. (*Angrily.*) But why did you leave yourself so vulnerable? What's the use of learning if it doesn't teach you to know yourself as you really are? (*Pause*). It's a pity your desert adventure couldn't have ended cleanly, in front of a firing squad. But that's for lesser enemies – not you. For you, killing wasn't enough. You had to be – destroyed. (*Stoops over* LAWRENCE.) The door at the bottom of the stairs through there is unlocked. It leads into the street.

The GENERAL *exits.* LAWRENCE, *painfully and slowly, begins to drag himself across the floor towards the other door. The lights fade.*

Scene Five

Scene: ALLENBY*'s field headquarters at Gaza. Before the lights come on we hear the sound of a military band playing a jaunty march, and the sound of voices and laughter.*

FRANKS (*in the darkness*). Hold it, General.

There is a flash from the darkness, and the sound of general laughter. ALLENBY, STORRS, BARRINGTON, FRANKS, *in the uniform of a war correspondent, and a* PHOTOGRAPHER *are all present. Everyone seems very jovial. An* AUSTRALIAN SOLDIER *on sentry duty stands in the outer entrance.*

I think, if you don't mind, General, just one more. And this time can we, perhaps, have a slightly more triumphant expression.

The PHOTOGRAPHER *changes the plate slide.*

ALLENBY. What? More triumphant? I thought I'd made myself odiously so in that one.

FRANKS. Forgive me, sir, but you really didn't look as if you'd just won a great battle.

ALLENBY. How does one look as if one had just won a great
battle? What do you suggest, Storrs?

STORRS. A rather bored and impassive expression, sir, as
if taking Jerusalem was something that happened to you
every day.

FRANKS. No, no. Not bored. Impassive, if you like, but stern
and unyielding and – well – victorious. Now shall we try
again, sir? (*To* PHOTOGRAPHER.) Ready?

The PHOTOGRAPHER *nods. The* ADC *enters.*

ADC (*to* ALLENBY). The drinks are ready, sir.

FRANKS. Just one moment, please.

An ORDERLY *enters with a tray of drinks which he places
on the table and exits.*

(*To* ALLENBY.) Just a little to the left. That's right. Now –
can we try that expression?

ALLENBY (*muttering*). Oh God, this is agony.

FRANKS. It won't last very long, sir.

ALLENBY *tries an unyielding expression.*

No. That isn't quite right.

STORRS. Of course a backcloth of Jerusalem would help.
And what about some Turkish prisoners, lying on the floor
in chains.

ALLENBY. Careful, Storrs. That appointment isn't official yet.

FRANKS. What appointment is that?

ALLENBY. Military Governor of Jerusalem.

FRANKS. Oh. Good. (*To* STORRS.) We must take a
photograph of you.

STORRS (*cowering*). Oh no.

ALLENBY (*laughing*). Oh yes. And get him to look
gubernatorial.

FRANKS (*patiently*). Now, sir. Can we try again?

ALLENBY *poses*.

Now think of Jerusalem.

ALLENBY (*through his teeth*). Jerusalem I've got. I'm thinking of Damascus.

BARRINGTON (*admiring his expression*). Very good, sir. That has the real Wellington look.

ALLENBY. Quiet, Brigadier – unless you want to be a Colonel again.

BARRINGTON (*aggrieved*). I meant it seriously, sir.

FRANKS. Hold it, General.

The flashlight is released again and the photograph taken.
ALLENBY *relaxes with relief.*

I think if you don't mind, General – just one more.

ALLENBY. No, certainly not. (*Pointing to a tray of drinks.*) Go in, gentlemen, have a drink and then leave me to fight my war.

BARRINGTON *and* STORRS *go towards the tray, where the* ADC *pours them drinks. The* PHOTOGRAPHER *packs up his apparatus.*

FRANKS (*taking out a notebook and pencil*). There's not very much more of your war left to fight, is there, General?

ALLENBY (*sharply*). There certainly is, and please don't give people at home any other impression. The Turkish Army is by no means beaten. It's suffered a defeat, but it's retiring in good order. There are many more battles to come and they'll become increasingly harder as the Turks shorten their lines of communication.

PHOTOGRAPHER (*at door*). Will that be all, Mr Franks?

FRANKS. Yes. Thank you. (*As* PHOTOGRAPHER *prepares to leave.*) Just a moment. (*To* ALLENBY.) We've rigged up a makeshift studio next door. Is there any hope of enticing you there tomorrow?

ALLENBY. I'm afraid I'm far too busy.

FRANKS. Pity. (*To* PHOTOGRAPHER.) All right.

PHOTOGRAPHER (*to* ALLENBY). Good afternoon, sir.

ALLENBY. Good day.

The PHOTOGRAPHER *exits.*

FRANKS. I've just one last request, sir.

ALLENBY. Come in. Have a whisky and soda while you make it.

They join BARRINGTON *and* STORRS. *The* ADC *pours drinks.*

FRANKS. My editor is very anxious for me to get an interview with Major Lawrence.

ALLENBY. I've no doubt he is.

FRANKS. Could I have your authority?

ALLENBY. My authority over Lawrence is sketchy, at the best of times. As regards an interview – even with you – I should say it was non-existent. Do you agree, Storrs?

STORRS. I would imagine that it might be rather easier for Mr Franks to get an interview with the Dalai Lama.

ALLENBY. Besides, when last heard from he was at Deraa, some hundred and fifty miles behind the enemy lines.

BARRINGTON. No, sir. He's here. Didn't you know?

ALLENBY (*bewildered*). Here?

BARRINGTON. Yes, sir. I saw him in the outer office about an hour ago. He was waiting to see you, he said. I'm sorry, sir, I thought you must have been told.

ALLENBY (*to* ADC). Did you know?

ADC. No, sir.

ALLENBY. Well, go and get him at once.

ADC. Yes, sir.

He goes out.

ALLENBY. Lawrence waiting? Usually he doesn't even knock. I look up and he's standing facing me. (*To* STORRS.) I'd have thought he'd have let you know, at least.

STORRS (*shrugging*). I never speculate about Laurence. It's unfruitful.

ALLENBY. Anyway he's here, which is the main thing, and he couldn't have come at a better time. I suppose he knew exactly when I'd take Jerusalem, although God knows, I didn't. The man's prescience is satanic.

FRANKS. May I stay, sir, for a moment?

ALLENBY. Of course. I doubt if it'll be much use to you. Storrs, have the other half.

STORRS. No, thank you, sir.

ADC (*opening the door*). Major Lawrence, sir.

LAWRENCE *comes in, walking with a limp that he is evidently at pains to conceal. He is in Arab clothes.*

ALLENBY. Why didn't you let me know you were here?

LAWRENCE. I understood you were busy with the press.

ALLENBY (*with a glance at* FRANKS). Ah. I see. This gentleman is the culprit. Mr Franks – Major Lawrence.

LAWRENCE (*politely*). How do you do.

STORRS. Hullo, T. E.

LAWRENCE. Hullo.

BARRINGTON. Hullo, Lawrence. Have you hurt yourself? You're limping a bit.

LAWRENCE. An accident with a camel. I got dragged through some barbed wire.

ALLENBY (*mischievously*). I think Mr Franks has a request to make of you, Lawrence.

LAWRENCE (*turning politely to* FRANKS). Oh really?

FRANKS (*nervously*). Well – Major – we war correspondents have our duty to perform like everyone else – so don't be too harsh with me. The public interest about you at home has become pretty intense lately and colourful figures are rare enough in this war, and – (*Glancing nervously at* ALLENBY *and* STORRS, *who are plainly enjoying their anticipation of* LAWRENCE's *response*.) Well, I suppose I'd better come straight out with it. Can I have an interview?

LAWRENCE. Yes. When?

FRANKS. Well – tomorrow.

LAWRENCE. What time?

FRANKS. Any time that would suit you. Ten o'clock?

LAWRENCE. Yes. Where?

FRANKS. Well, anywhere, but of course, what would be far the best would be if you would come along to the studio I've rigged up – and then we could get some really beautiful photographs.

LAWRENCE. Where is your studio?

FRANKS (*hardly able to believe his luck*). Next door to here.

ALLENBY (*with a slightly worried frown*). He has backcloths at his studio.

FRANKS (*writing feverishly*). Oh, General, you go on far too much about those backcloths. A photographic cloth can be quite plain, you know. Would you allow yourself to be photographed in front of a backcloth?

LAWRENCE. Whatever you think best.

FRANKS. Good. Oh, good. Ten o'clock, then?

LAWRENCE *nods*.

You're not going to let me down, are you?

LAWRENCE. No, I'll see you tomorrow.

FRANKS. Thank you, Major. (*To* ALLENBY.) Afternoon, sir. (*To the others*.) Goodbye.

He goes. STORRS, *conscious of an atmosphere, hastily finishes his drink.*

STORRS. We'd better leave you too, sir.

ALLENBY (*looking at* LAWRENCE). If you would.

STORRS (*casually to* LAWRENCE). I hope I shall see something of you while you're here.

LAWRENCE. I won't be here long.

STORRS (*to* ALLENBY). Goodbye, sir. (*Goes.*)

BARRINGTON. Could I have just two words with Lawrence, sir? Rather important.

ALLENBY *nods.* BARRINGTON *turns to* LAWRENCE.

I've had a rather sharp inquiry from the Foreign Office regarding the question of so-called atrocities on your front –

LAWRENCE. I have no front.

BARRINGTON. Well, during your raids and ambushes and things. It's been alleged through a neutral embassy that you don't take prisoners.

He awaits a response from LAWRENCE *who remains silent.*

An official denial from you would help enormously.

LAWRENCE (*politely*). Then you shall have it.

BARRINGTON. Good. Would you let me have it tomorrow, in writing?

LAWRENCE. In writing?

BARRINGTON *nods.*

Very well.

BARRINGTON. Thank you. (*Turns to go.*)

LAWRENCE. The Arabs have been less demanding. My denials to them on more important issues are confined to the verbal.

BARRINGTON (*stopping short*). You mean the denial would be untrue?

LAWRENCE. Not entirely untrue. Misleading is a better word. We do take prisoners – when we are not being chased, and can spare the men to escort them to Feisal and I've managed to keep some control of the situation. A combination of those contingencies is unhappily rare.

BARRINGTON. But this admission is very serious.

LAWRENCE (*raising his voice slightly*). I agree. Did the neutral embassy have anything to say about the Turkish treatment of Arab prisoners?

BARRINGTON. No, but if there have been reprisals…

LAWRENCE (*with a sharp laugh*). Reprisals? The old game of who started it? Who's to know? And does it matter? All I can tell you is that for a long time now no wounded Arab soldier has been left on the field for the Turks to take. If we can't move him we shoot him.

BARRINGTON (*hotly*). Listen, Lawrence – the Turk's a clean fighter.

LAWRENCE. I've no doubt, Colonel, but ours isn't a clean war. It's an Asiatic revolution, and a European who tries to direct the course of such a thing is apt to find himself rather out of his depth.

BARRINGTON. But – are you suggesting…?

ALLENBY (*interposing*). That's enough, Barrington. You can see Lawrence tomorrow.

BARRINGTON. Yes, sir. (*Salutes punctiliously, turns on his heels and goes.*)

ALLENBY. Don't worry about that.

LAWRENCE. No, sir. I won't.

ALLENBY. You made it sound pretty grim, I must say.

LAWRENCE. I could have made it sound grimmer.

ALLENBY. Well, you've come at a good time.

LAWRENCE. Yes, sir. Congratulations.

ALLENBY. Thank you. Tell me, how did you get the news?

LAWRENCE. I didn't, until I reached here.

ALLENBY. What did you come for, then?

LAWRENCE. I want to ask you to find me another job.

A pause.

ALLENBY. What other job?

LAWRENCE. Any one at all, providing that it has nothing whatever to do with the Arab Revolt. I suppose, at a pinch, I could still draw you some quite useful maps.

ALLENBY (*nodding, at length*). I see. Go on.

LAWRENCE. Is my request granted?

ALLENBY. It may be. Tell me why you wish to relinquish your present post.

LAWRENCE. You're going to make it hard for me, are you?

ALLENBY (*quietly*). I see no reason to make it easy.

LAWRENCE. Yes. I admire you for that. You want my excuses for desertion?

ALLENBY. Your reasons.

LAWRENCE (*nodding appreciatively*). Very well. (*Quietly matter of fact.*) I have come to believe that the Arab Revolt is a fake, founded on deceit and sustained by lies, and I want no further part in it.

ALLENBY (*making notes*). I see. Go on.

LAWRENCE. On the military side I have only failure to report. The bridge at Yarmuk has not been blown and Arab forces have at no time successfully intervened in your campaign to date.

ALLENBY (*quietly, continuing writing*). Yes?

LAWRENCE. To sum up, the whole venture is morally, militarily and financially unjustifiable – a total washout, and should be abandoned. (*After a pause.*) Anyway, I can't go on.

He looks at ALLENBY, *who makes an impassive final note, laying down his pen.*

However, if you don't agree with what I've said about the Arab Revolt and want me to suggest someone to take my place...

ALLENBY (*quietly*). There is no one to take your place. Now, dealing with your points in reverse order and leaving out the last. (*Looking at his notes.*) Your military failure is untrue, even after taking into account your tendency for histrionic exaggeration. I haven't required Arab intervention yet in my campaign, and I don't expect you to succeed in blowing up every damn bridge I ask you to destroy. The Arab Revolt a fake? That's for you to say, but you told me once that you could will yourself into believing it wasn't.

LAWRENCE. I think it was you who told me. Anyway, my will has proved less trustworthy than I thought.

ALLENBY. What's happened, Lawrence?

LAWRENCE (*suddenly tired*). Can't we say battle weariness?

ALLENBY. No. Not for you.

LAWRENCE. Disillusionment, cowardice...

ALLENBY. No. Something extraordinary happened. What?

LAWRENCE. I had a vision. It happens to people in the desert.

ALLENBY. A vision of what?

LAWRENCE. Of the truth.

ALLENBY. About the Arab Revolt?

LAWRENCE. No. About myself.

ALLENBY. And the truth is – (*Tapping his notes.*) 'I can't go on'?

LAWRENCE. That's part of the truth.

ALLENBY. The most important part, isn't it?

LAWRENCE. No. Only the most relevant.

A pause.

ALLENBY (*suddenly*). What a pity! What an awful pity.

LAWRENCE *looks at the floor in silence.*

All right. I'll send you back to England.

LAWRENCE. I haven't asked for that.

STORRS *enters and whispers to the* SENTRY. HAMED *follows* STORRS *on.*

ALLENBY. The War Office should be glad to have you. You're due for promotion, so I'll appoint you Lieutenant Colonel. I've also recommended you – some weeks ago – for the DSO so with that and your CB and your wound stripes you should make quite a show there.

The SENTRY *comes forward and clicks his heels.*

Yes?

SENTRY. Mr Storrs is outside with an urgent telegram, sir.

ALLENBY. Send him in.

SENTRY. Yes, sir. (*Beckons to* STORRS.)

LAWRENCE *turns to go.*

ALLENBY. No, stay. I want a word with you about your successor.

STORRS *comes in. The* SENTRY *resumes his position.* HAMED *exits.*

STORRS (*handing* ALLENBY *a telegram*). Downing Street, sir. They want you to make a triumphal entry into Jerusalem on Wednesday.

ALLENBY. What do they think I am? A Roman Emperor?

STORRS. Brass bands, victory marches, beautiful girls hurling flowers at us. I'm looking forward to it. (*To* LAWRENCE.) Your man Hamed is outside. Wants to see you.

LAWRENCE. He should have gone. I ordered him back to Prince Feisal's camp two hours ago.

STORRS. Well, he's determined to talk to you. Seems very agitated. When are you going back, T. E.?

ALLENBY (*with sudden harshness*). He's not going back.

STORRS. What?

ALLENBY. He feels he can't go on any more. He's had all that flesh and blood will stand, I see his point. I'm sending him to the War Office.

LAWRENCE (*looking at the ground*). May I go, sir? I'm feeling tired. We can talk about my – successor some other time.

ALLENBY (*carelessly*). Very well. (*As* LAWRENCE *reaches the door*.) Just one moment. I shall want you to take part in this entry on Wednesday.

LAWRENCE. In what capacity?

ALLENBY. Chief British liaison officer to Arab forces in the field, of course.

LAWRENCE. No, sir.

ALLENBY (*coldly*; *it is an order*). You will march directly behind me, and attend all the various ceremonies at my side.

LAWRENCE (*with a sudden hard laugh*). Oh yes. Good textbook stuff. (*Indicating the telegram*.) A General should be ready at one instant to exploit any opportunity suddenly laid open to him.

ALLENBY (*coldly*). You seem to think my order is a punishment. It isn't. The honour that is being done to you on Wednesday is an award for your past. If it gives you uncomfortable thoughts about your present that's your affair, and not mine.

LAWRENCE (*now suddenly weary*). And that's from the same textbook, isn't it? How to deal with deserters. I've learnt how to deal with them too – but not from Sandhurst training. From experience. Sad, scared, broken-willed little creatures – you can't persuade them or threaten them or even joke them back into battle. But sometimes you can shame them back. It's surprising how often – if you use the right technique. You know, I think that I admire you more than any man on earth, and I've never admired you more than I do at this moment. On my way here I had worked out for myself every stratagem you might use to get me to go back, and had planned all my moves to counter them. And I'm beaten in five minutes. Can I see my bodyguard? Storrs says he's outside.

ALLENBY (*calling*). Sentry!

SENTRY (*appearing*). Sir?

ALLENBY. Get Major Lawrence's Arab servant.

SENTRY. Yes, sir.

He moves upstage, whistles softly and beckons off.

LAWRENCE. I suppose what I left out of account is the splendid core of cruelty that all great Generals should have.

HAMED *comes in.*

Hamed, why are you still in Gaza? I ordered you back to Prince Feisal's camp two hours ago. Is that not so?

HAMED (*murmuring*). It is so, el Aurans.

LAWRENCE. Why then have you disobeyed me?

HAMED. My camel has died.

LAWRENCE. She seemed all right this morning.

HAMED. A sudden illness must have struck her, el Aurans.

LAWRENCE. Yes. Very sudden. There was my camel...

HAMED (*looking at the ground*). She has died too.

LAWRENCE. Of the same illness?

HAMED. Assuredly. (*Looking up at* LAWRENCE.) So now I must stay with you, here, el Aurans. There is now no means of leaving you, is there?

LAWRENCE. Until you find another camel.

HAMED. In Gaza they are hard to find.

LAWRENCE. By Thursday morning, you must have found two new camels –

HAMED. Two?

LAWRENCE. – two fine, fast camels every bit as good as those you have just got rid of.

HAMED (*his face lighting up with joy*). In an hour –

LAWRENCE. Listen. Thursday at the first light of dawn. (*With a look at* ALLENBY.) On Wednesday I have a duty to perform in Jerusalem.

HAMED. This is not a joke?

LAWRENCE. No.

HAMED. But you said –

LAWRENCE. You should not always confuse what I say with what I do.

    HAMED *bows suddenly to* LAWRENCE, *takes his hand, kisses it, and then places it on his head, Arab fashion. Then he turns and goes out quickly.* LAWRENCE *shrugs his shoulders, facing* ALLENBY.

    Well, sir, I told you my will isn't what it was.

ALLENBY. I think it'll mend.

LAWRENCE. No. I'll have to try and find a substitute. (*Turning away*.) But there are just two things I wish you knew.

ALLENBY. What?

LAWRENCE. The kind of deserter you're sending back. And the kind of battle you're sending him back to –

    LAWRENCE *goes*.

STORRS (*after a pause*). You'd have made as good a diplomat as a soldier.

ALLENBY. I deserve the insult.

STORRS. No insult. But were you right to get him to go back?

ALLENBY (*angrily*). Am I supposed to care about what's right? It was necessary. That's all that concerns me. (*Unhappily*.) All that ought to concern me. (*Gets up and goes to pour himself a drink. With a sigh*.) Oh God, Storrs, won't it be wonderful when this damned war's over.

    The lights fade.

Scene Six

In the darkness we hear the distant rumble of heavy gunfire.

Scene: outside LAWRENCE's *tent near the village of Tafas.*
LAWRENCE *himself is shaving, using a canvas basin and a
mirror hung up on a pole.* FLIGHT-LIEUTENANT HIGGINS
*comes out of the tent with some pages of typescript in his hand.
The gunfire continues throughout the scene.*

HIGGINS. I've done it, sir. I hope I've got it all right. Would
you check it as soon as possible?

LAWRENCE. Does your pilot want to take off?

HIGGINS. Well – it's getting a bit late, sir, and the C-in-C is
waiting for this. Highest priority.

LAWRENCE. Read it.

HIGGINS (*reading*). 'Operations of 25th and 26th September,
1918. I decided to place the main Arab force in the direct
path of the Turkish Fourth Army's line of retreat. My staff
considered this a hazardous enterprise, in view of the fact
that the Fourth Army was retreating intact to cover
Damascus. They thought that our untried force, outnumbered
by roughly four to one, might prove no match for disciplined
troops. I, on the other hand, reckoned that the element of
surprise would outweigh this disadvantage. I am glad to
report that events have justified my unweary optimism.'

LAWRENCE. 'Unweary'? This report has enough hubris in it
without your adding to it. I said 'unwary'.

HIGGINS (*brightly*). Oh. Sorry, sir. Unwary. (*Makes a
correction.*) And what was the other word you used?
Hu-something?

LAWRENCE. Hubris. It's the Greek for showing-off.

HIGGINS. Oh but, sir – I mean – surely you've got something
(*Indicating report.*) to show off about, I'd say.

LAWRENCE. You think so?

HIGGINS. The Turks caught in a trap between our chaps in the
south and your chaps up here. I mean it's bloody marvellous,
sir. (*There is no reply.*) Bloody marvellous. (*Continuing to*

read.) 'I am happy to report that the Fourth Turkish Army has, since eleven hundred hours this morning, ceased to exist. A detailed report of the operation follows...'

LAWRENCE (*interrupting*). Very well. As I have your sanction for hubris, you might as well add this to the main report. After 'ceased to exist' –

HIGGINS *has his pencil and pad*.

'In view of this situation it is my intention to enter the City of Damascus at first light tomorrow and to hold it in the name and authority of Prince Feisal. I assume this action will meet with your approval – an assumption forced on me by the fact that should it not – it will anyway be too late for you to inform me.'

HIGGINS. My gosh, I'll be able to write my memoirs after the war. *Lawrence of Arabia and I* by S. R. Higgins.

LAWRENCE (*interrupting*). Did you invent that name?

HIGGINS. What? Higgins?

LAWRENCE. No. The other one.

HIGGINS. 'Lawrence of Arabia'? Good heavens, no, sir. That's what the press have been calling you for months.

LAWRENCE. Have they? I didn't know.

HIGGINS. Shall I read the detailed stuff, sir?

LAWRENCE. No. You'd better take off. Was there anything that seemed wrong to you in it?

HIGGINS (*doubtfully*). No. Well there was just one thing... (*Breaks off, looking rather scared*.)

LAWRENCE. What's that?

HIGGINS. The night raid on that station.

LAWRENCE. What about it?

HIGGINS. There's something in it – I wonder if it's wise to – I mean it is an official report.

LAWRENCE. Well, read it.

HIGGINS (*reading*). 'Operations of September 18th. In order to complete the encirclement of Deraa... a night assault on the railway... surprise not wholly achieved...' Ah. Here we are, sir. 'Ordering the Zaali to give covering fire I went down the embankment with my personal bodyguard and laid charges. These were successfully detonated and the bridge destroyed but, the enemy now directed his fire at the bridge, my companion being badly hit at the first burst. I attempted to drag him up the embankment but without success and, as the Turks were beginning to issue from their blockhouse, I had no recourse but to leave him, after carrying out the usual practice in such cases. I rejoined the troop, and the retirement was completed without further loss.'

He stops. LAWRENCE *is looking at the ground.*

LAWRENCE (*presently*). What part specifically do you object to?

HIGGINS. Well, sir, the implication.

LAWRENCE. That I killed the man that was wounded?

HIGGINS. Yes, sir.

LAWRENCE. But I did kill him.

HIGGINS (*shocked*). Oh. Well... (*Defiantly.*) But it's not the kind of thing you say in an official report.

LAWRENCE. Isn't it? I describe later on how we killed four thousand Turks.

HIGGINS (*horrified*). Yes – but they're the enemy and this is one of your own men.

LAWRENCE. Yes.

HIGGINS. Of course, I know he was only an Arab, but still it does sound – do forgive me, sir – a bit – callous.

LAWRENCE. I see. And you'd like me to make it sound less callous?

HIGGINS. I really think you should take it out altogether, sir. I mean, there might be trouble with his wife or something –

LAWRENCE. He didn't have a wife. He once had a friend, but he's dead too.

HIGGINS (*a little cross at* LAWRENCE'*s lack of imagination*). Well, I'm sure he must have had someone who'll care about his death –

LAWRENCE. Yes, he did. But I doubt if that person will give much trouble.

HIGGINS. Well, you never know, sir. Anyway, have I your permission to edit the passage a little? I could just say the burst of machine-gun fire missed you but killed him instantly.

LAWRENCE (*politely*). A very happy invention.

HIGGINS. I'll do it when I get to HQ. Goodbye, sir.

LAWRENCE (*getting up*). Goodbye.

AUDA ABU TAYI *strides on. He looks angry, hot and weary. His clothes are torn and bloodstained.*

AUDA. Who would have thought the day would come when Auda would grow tired of killing Turks? (*Throws down his rifle.*) Old age is a terrible thing.

HIGGINS (*to* LAWRENCE). Well, sir, I'll be off.

AUDA (*squinting venomously at* HIGGINS). By Allah! A Turk. (*Picks up his rifle.*)

LAWRENCE. No. No – British.

AUDA (*accusingly*). I know the British uniform. That is a Turk.

LAWRENCE. He's an officer in King George's Air Force. (*To* HIGGINS.) You'd better clear off. He thinks you're the enemy.

HIGGINS. Oh Lord! – I say – what a scruffy-looking old wog, or is he one of your Generals?

LAWRENCE. Yes. That's exactly what he is.

HIGGINS. Gosh! Poor old Higgins. Always putting his foot in it. Well – goodbye, sir.

HIGGINS salutes LAWRENCE, turns and meets AUDA's darkly suspicious gaze. Rather nervously he salutes him too, then exits.

AUDA (*wearily*). Well, my friend, is it over?

LAWRENCE. Yes.

AUDA. Tomorrow – Damascus?

LAWRENCE. Yes.

AUDA. Our enemy destroyed and the dream of two years fulfilled. Damascus! Allah indeed is good.

LAWRENCE. Allah is good.

Pause. AUDA looks at LAWRENCE with thoughtful and sympathetic eyes.

AUDA. They have told me about Hamed.

LAWRENCE. I would not have told you.

AUDA. I am the one you should have told.

LAWRENCE. It's not a tale that should be told to a friend.

AUDA. Who else but a friend?

LAWRENCE. An enemy – or a stranger. To anyone but a friend.

AUDA (*gently*). Let us speak of other things. Let us speak of yesterday's great battle.

A pause.

LAWRENCE. Did you know he opened his eyes for a moment when I lifted my pistol. He had them tightly closed until that moment. He was in great pain. But it was the will of fate that he should open his eyes and see me pointing the pistol at his head. He said 'Rashid will be angry with you, el Aurans.'

AUDA. I remember Rashid. He died on our march in the desert.

LAWRENCE. Yes. The day I failed with my compass. So then I said, 'Salute Rashid from me,' and he smiled. Then the pain came back and he closed his eyes again. Just as I was lifting the revolver once more to his head he said, 'God will give you peace.' Then I fired. The Turks were already coming out of the blockhouse.

A pause.

AUDA. The memory of it will not always be so sharp.

LAWRENCE. I once said the same to Hamed. He didn't believe it then and nor do I now.

AUDA. You must think of other things. Think of Damascus and what we must do there.

LAWRENCE. Yes.

AUDA. And all that we must do after Damascus, for only now does our fight truly begin. (*Anxiously.*) You will go on fighting with us and for us, el Aurans? For Allah knows we will need you in peace even more than we have in war.

LAWRENCE. Yes. I suppose I must try and make amends.

AUDA. Amends?

LAWRENCE. To the people I've misled.

A pause.

AUDA. By Allah, I think your victories have made you mad. Have you misled us all from Mecca to Damascus – a thousand miles and more – against an enemy many times our strength?

LAWRENCE. Forgive me, Auda. It was a feeble joke.

AUDA. You will fight for us in peace as you fought for us in war?

LAWRENCE. Yes. To the limits of my strength. Can I say more?

AUDA. No. For what limits are there to the strength of el Aurans?

LAWRENCE. Some, I think.

AUDA. None, I know. (*Embraces* LAWRENCE.) I have lost many sons – yes, and grandsons – but for none of them did I grieve so much as I did for you that day when you left us and went to Gaza and we thought you had gone for ever. What time tonight?

LAWRENCE. Midnight. We shall be in Damascus by dawn.

BARRINGTON *enters hurriedly.*

BARRINGTON. Ah, Lawrence. Good. I'm glad I've found you. You really ought to leave clearer indications about the exact site of your headquarters.

AUDA, *under the stress of an evidently stormy emotion, clutches* BARRINGTON's *tunic, and pulls him to him.*

AUDA. Who are you?

BARRINGTON. My name's Barrington. General Barrington – GHQ.

AUDA (*fiercely*). Tell them, GHQ, tell them in England what I Auda Abu Tayi say of el Aurans. Of Manhood – (*Shakes* BARRINGTON.) the man. Of Freedom – (*Shakes him again.*) free. A spirit – (*Shakes him a third time.*) without equal. I see no flaw in him. And if any offal-eating traitor should ever deny the greatness of that man – (*Pointing to* LAWRENCE.) may the curse of Auda fall upon his dung-filled head.

He shakes BARRINGTON *a fourth time, then releases him abruptly, picks up his rifle and strides out.*

BARRINGTON. One of your chaps?

LAWRENCE. Yes.

BARRINGTON. The Bedouin are excitable people. Far too excitable.

LAWRENCE. How did you get up here?

BARRINGTON. By armoured car from Deraa. I was with the Fourth Cavalry Division when they entered the town this morning. The GOC sent me here to find you and bring you down there to him at once.

LAWRENCE. Oh? Under arrest?

BARRINGTON (*impatiently*). No, of course not, but he's raging – absolutely raging – and God knows – after the sights I saw this morning I don't blame him. Apparently some of your wogs sneaked into the place last night…

LAWRENCE. May we make our language more official, General? A contingent of Prince Feisal's Arab forces, acting under my orders, last night captured the important road and rail centre of Deraa –

BARRINGTON. Yes, I've no doubt that's how it'll go down in your report. Listen, I'm a fairly hardened soldier, Lawrence, but in all my life I've never seen anything like it. It's utterly sickening. They're burning and looting everything Turkish they can find. It's utterly sickening. They're massacring the garrison – there are only a handful of survivors. We've even had to surround the military hospital. It's a very dangerous situation and, as you seem to be the only person who can control these savages, you've got to come down with me now at once...

LAWRENCE (*coldly*). I'm sorry, sir, but I'm afraid I can't spare the time.

A pause.

BARRINGTON (*wide-eyed*). Shall I report that to the GOC?

LAWRENCE. You will anyway, so why ask me? You can also tell the GOC that I suggest he orders his troops out of a town which was captured and is now being securely held by mine. And now – sir – if you don't mind – I have an important operation planned for tonight, and I must prepare for it.

He turns to go. BARRINGTON *runs to bar his way.*

BARRINGTON. I'm getting pretty tired of these schoolboy jokes of yours, Lawrence.

LAWRENCE (*amused*). Schoolboy jokes? How interesting. I've grown up a bit since we first met at Abdullah's camp. Or hadn't you noticed?

BARRINGTON. Your suggestion is serious?

LAWRENCE *shrugs.*

That Deraa be left in the hands of those savages?

LAWRENCE (*quietly*). It may be that some of those savages come from a village called Tafas. We followed the Turks into it two days ago. Just outside the village we saw a child with a bayonet wound in his neck – but he was still alive. When I bent over him, he screamed 'Don't hit me, Baba.' Then he ran away from us until he fell over and died. That was only the first thing we saw. Then we went into the village. After we had seen the bodies of eighteen women, all bayoneted obscenely, two of them pregnant, I said 'The best of you brings me the most Turkish dead'. I note, with interest, sir, that my wishes were apparently carried out last night in Deraa. (*A thought striking him.*) In Deraa? How stupid! I hadn't realised. In Deraa? (*Laughs softly and makes a move to go.*)

BARRINGTON (*forcibly restraining him*). Are you quite lost to all human feeling?

LAWRENCE (*laughing again, with now a different note*). Do you know, General, I think you're right That's exactly what I am. (*His laugh grows louder, with a shade of hysteria in it.*) Quite lost to all human feeling.

BARRINGTON (*appalled*). You're a callous, soulless, sadistic little brute.

LAWRENCE (*still laughing, eagerly*). Yes, yes, oh yes. Especially soulless.

BARRINGTON. You sicken me.

He pushes LAWRENCE *away violently so that he falls down, still laughing, but weakly now.* BARRINGTON *goes out.*

LAWRENCE (*calling after him*). I sicken myself. That's the joke. Not a schoolboy joke. Just – a – joke. (*The laughter is no longer laughter, but the sound continues.*) Lawrence of Arabia – the soulless wonder...

Suddenly a quiet, clear voice – actual not recorded – cuts through the sound that LAWRENCE *is making.*

HAMED'S VOICE. God will give you peace.

LAWRENCE (*struggling to his feet*). No, Hamed, never. Never in this life. (*Exits unsteadily.*)

HAMED'S VOICE (*as* LAWRENCE *disappears*). God will give you peace.

The lights fade.

Scene Seven

*Loud and clear comes a bugle call, playing the reveille. The
lights come up.*

Scene: FLIGHT-LIEUTENANT STOKER*'s office. He is sitting
at the desk, looking up in bewilderment at an* RAF CORPORAL.

FLIGHT-LIEUTENANT. What? But I don't understand. The
Group Captain coming to see me? Are you sure?

CORPORAL. On his way, sir.

FLIGHT-LIEUTENANT. But why didn't he tell me to come
and see him?

CORPORAL. Don't know, sir.

FLIGHT-LIEUTENANT. Well, it's very odd. Thank you.

*He begins hastily to clear up his desk, moving a few
documents from the 'In' tray to the 'Out' tray, and emptying
an overfull ashtray. There is a peremptory knock. Nervously.*

Come in.

The GROUP CAPTAIN *comes in. He is only half-dressed
and looks dishevelled and harassed. The* CORPORAL
springs to attention.

GROUP CAPTAIN. Corporal – tell the Flight-Sergeant of
B Flight to report to me here immediately.

CORPORAL. Yes, sir. (*Goes out.*)

FLIGHT-LIEUTENANT. Why, sir. This is a surprise. I don't
often have the honour…

GROUP CAPTAIN (*hoarsely*). Do you keep any drink here?

FLIGHT-LIEUTENANT. A little – er – medicinal, sir.

*He opens a cupboard and takes out a bottle of whisky and
a glass and pours a drink.*

GROUP CAPTAIN. I need it. My office has become a
nightmare. The telephone hasn't stopped since six this
morning, when the duty officer woke me with the news.
(*Taking the glass and drinking.*) Thanks. Now I'm not at all

sure it isn't being tapped. Probably the *Daily Mirror*. They were the first on. (*Takes another swig and hands the glass back to the bewildered* FLIGHT-LIEUTENANT.) Now, listen, we've got to get this fellow off the station within an hour...

FLIGHT-LIEUTENANT. Which fellow?

GROUP CAPTAIN (*impatiently*). Ross, of course. Air Ministry are most insistent that there aren't any photographs, so I suggest we smuggle him through my private gate. Agreed?

FLIGHT-LIEUTENANT. Er – excuse me, sir, I'm just the least little bit behind. Do I agree that we smuggle Aircraftman Ross off the station, through your own private gate? That was the question, wasn't it?

GROUP CAPTAIN. Oh, my God! You don't know? No, I suppose you wouldn't. We're trying to keep it as dark as possible, though everyone will know tonight –

FLIGHT-LIEUTENANT (*patiently*). Has it anything to do with the charge I put him on for hearing by you this morning?

GROUP CAPTAIN. You put him on a charge?

FLIGHT-LIEUTENANT. Yes, sir. Gross insubordination.

GROUP CAPTAIN. Who to?

FLIGHT-LIEUTENANT. Me.

A pause.

GROUP CAPTAIN (*solicitously*). I think you'd better have a nip of your own whisky.

FLIGHT-LIEUTENANT (*virtuously*). Never touch it in the morning.

GROUP CAPTAIN. Well, I will. (*Muttering.*) A charge? God. If the *Mirror* got hold of that. (*Takes another glass from the* FLIGHT-LIEUTENANT.) You know who it was you've charged with insubordination? Lawrence of Arabia.

FLIGHT-LIEUTENANT (*after a pause, confidently*). Oh no. Oh no. That can't be. I mean...

GROUP CAPTAIN. How exactly was he insubordinate?

FLIGHT-LIEUTENANT. He was late on pass. I asked him who he'd been with, that night. He said the Archbishop of Canterbury – (*His voice begins to falter.*) Lord and Lady Astor, and Mr and Mrs George Bernard... Oh, my God!

GROUP CAPTAIN (*holding out the bottle*). Here.

FLIGHT-LIEUTENANT (*taking it*). But it's unbelievable. Why has he done it?

GROUP CAPTAIN. Well, that's the question. It's very difficult to get anything out of him. I had an hour with him, nearly. A bit awkward. I had to ask him to sit, of course.

FLIGHT-LIEUTENANT. Of course.

GROUP CAPTAIN. Kept on using the one word, refuge. The RAF was his refuge.

FLIGHT-LIEUTENANT. From what?

GROUP CAPTAIN. God knows. From himself and his reputation, he said. He wanted a number, not a name. Very insistent about his number. Lets him lose his identity. One of a mass. Fellow's a bit screwy, if you ask me.

FLIGHT-LIEUTENANT (*excitedly*). It wouldn't be a public protest about the Arabs being let down at Versailles?

GROUP CAPTAIN. No. Asked him that.

FLIGHT-LIEUTENANT. Or the Palestine Question?

GROUP CAPTAIN. No. Welcomes a Jewish State. (*Takes out a piece of paper.*) He fought for – er – just a minute – I've got it here. Yes, here it is. (*Reading.*) He 'fought for the whole Semitic race, irrespective of religion.' He has no grievance at all about either Arabia or Palestine. 'Churchill's recent settlement of the Middle East has brought us out with clean hands.' Those were his exact words.

FLIGHT-LIEUTENANT. Really? His exact words?

GROUP CAPTAIN (*glowering*). Yes – and don't you quote them.

FLIGHT-LIEUTENANT. No, sir.

GROUP CAPTAIN. Queer little fellow. If he wasn't who he is, you might feel quite sorry for him.

FLIGHT-LIEUTENANT. What's going to happen to him?

GROUP CAPTAIN. The Air Ministry are turning him out pronto. They're flaming mad. They're being badgered already by foreign embassies. Going to be questions in the House too. Oh, no. I mean, you can't have the Service turned into a rest home for war heroes. Army chap, too.

FLIGHT-LIEUTENANT. Legally *can* they turf him out?

GROUP CAPTAIN. Oh yes. Entered under false name and false particulars. (*Holds out glass*.) Here.

FLIGHT-LIEUTENANT (*taking the glass*). Thank you, sir.

There is a knock on the door.

Come in.

The FLIGHT-SERGEANT *comes in and salutes.*

FLIGHT-SERGEANT (*roaring*). Flight-Sergeant Thompson, B Flight, reporting, sir.

GROUP CAPTAIN. Yes, Flight. It's about a man in your Flight. Aircraftman Ross.

FLIGHT-SERGEANT. Yes, sir.

GROUP CAPTAIN. He has to be off this station within an hour.

FLIGHT-SERGEANT. Yes, sir.

GROUP CAPTAIN. You knew about it?

FLIGHT-SERGEANT. He told me, sir.

GROUP CAPTAIN. Did he tell you why?

FLIGHT-SERGEANT. Yes, sir.

GROUP CAPTAIN. Oh. Well, don't tell the rest of the Flight.

FLIGHT-SERGEANT. They all know, sir, I told them.

GROUP CAPTAIN. Oh. my God! (*To* FLIGHT-LIEUTENANT.) It'll be all round the camp by now –

FLIGHT-LIEUTENANT (*to* FLIGHT-SERGEANT, *curiously*). Exactly what did he tell you, Flight?

FLIGHT-SERGEANT. What the Group Captain said to him, sir. That he was the wrong type for the RAF. Didn't fit in. Was too old. Couldn't do the job – so he was being hoof – discharged the Service.

A pause.

FLIGHT-LIEUTENANT. That's all he told you, Flight?

FLIGHT-SERGEANT. Yes, sir.

GKOUP CAPTAIN. Nothing else at all?

FLIGHT-SERGEANT (*trying to remember*). No, sir. Except that he didn't know what he was going to do with himself now, sir.

GROUP CAPTAIN. That's all right, Flight. (*Dismissing him.*) Thank you.

FLIGHT-SERGEANT. Leave to speak, sir. (*The* GROUP CAPTAIN *nods*). I've known this airman ten weeks. He's not an ideal recruit, but then who is? In fact he's not a bad little b-chap at all. I think – if you only let him stay, sir – I can see to it that he won't get into no more trouble. And I'm sure, some day, he'll make an airman.

A pause.

GROUP CAPTAIN. I'm sorry, Flight – but it's all settled.

FLIGHT-LIEUTENANT (*with a faint smile*). He doesn't fit in.

FLIGHT-SERGEANT. Yes, sir. It's just that it takes all sorts, sir – that's what I always say –

GROUP CAPTAIN (*sharply*). That's enough, Flight. See that he's off the station by nine hundred hours –

FLIGHT-SERGEANT. Yes, sir. (*Salutes, marches to the door and turns.*) Forgive forthrightness, sir. It's just I don't believe there's anyone in this world who can't be made to fit in somehow –

GROUP CAPTAIN. Yes, Flight.

FLIGHT-SERGEANT. Trust I have given no offence.

GROUP CAPTAIN. No offence. It's just that Ross happens to be a special case. A very special case.

FLIGHT-SERGEANT. Yes, sir.

He salutes and goes. The lights fade.

Scene Eight

Scene: the Hut at the Depot. LAWRENCE, *in civilian clothes, is packing a kitbag. A bugle is heard off.* EVANS *enters.*

EVANS (*embarrassed, but with false joviality*). Hullo, Rossie, boy. How's the world?

LAWRENCE. All right. Break on?

EVANS. Yes.

LAWRENCE. No cocoa and biscuits this morning?

EVANS. Not hungry. Rossie… (*Holds out some money.*)

LAWRENCE. No. You keep that.

EVANS. Oh, but I couldn't. (*Puts the money on the bed.*) You'll be needing it more than me now, anyway.

LAWRENCE (*realising resistance is useless*). Thank you, Taff. I must give you back the half crown.

EVANS (*as* LAWRENCE *holds it out*). Keep it, man. No, keep it. It's not much, but it could help out there.

LAWRENCE. Thank you, Taff.

EVANS. What are you going to do?

LAWRENCE (*putting the money away*). No idea, Taff.

EVANS. Got a job to go to?

LAWRENCE. No.

EVANS. It's terrible this unemployment. Terrible. I wouldn't be in this place if it weren't for that, I can tell you. No fear. You got a girl?

LAWRENCE. No.

EVANS (*smiling*). Lucky man.

LAWRENCE. Yes. I suppose so.

EVANS. One comfort, too – you don't have to tell her you got hoofed. Anyone to tell?

LAWRENCE. No.

EVANS. I'll write to anyone if you'll give me the address. Say what bad luck it was you got on the wrong side of the Station Commander. Just unreasonable, I'll say he was.

PARSONS *comes in quickly followed by* DICKINSON.

PARSONS. Listen – I don't want no no's about this, because I've talked to all the others except Taff here – and he'll say yes like the rest, I know – won't you, Taff?

EVANS (*plaintively*). I don't know what it is, yet.

PARSONS (*snarling*). I'm telling you, aren't I?

EVANS. Sorry.

PARSONS. We're writing a document – quite dignified – most respectful – dear sir – we have the honour – all that cock – and we're all signing it and sending it to the Group Captain – and what we're going to say is that we all think that the way they're treating you is the most dirtiest, bleedingest trick that even those bastards have ever pulled on one of us – and that's saying something.

LAWRENCE (*quietly*). On one of us?

PARSONS. Yes, that's right, but of course – what I said just now – we gotta make it respectful – B Flight suggest there has been some slight misapprehension regarding Airman Ross not fitting in – (*Warming to his subject.*) because if he can fit into B Flight he can bloody well fit into the RAF or into any other bloody Service you can bloody well think of –

sir. (*Thoughtfully.*) Trouble is, we're really going to need you to write this for us. Got the time?

LAWRENCE. No. Besides you mustn't send it.

PARSONS. Don't worry. We're sending it. Aren't we, Taff?

EVANS. I'm game – if all the others are. Are they really, Sailor?

PARSONS (*fiercely*). What kind of a mug do you think I am? In this sort of lark it's all or no one – see. One single blackleg – just one, and they'll beat us. There aren't no blacklegs on this.

LAWRENCE. Dickinson?

PARSONS. He's in. Thinks it's a joke, mind you, hasn't got no proper social conscience – officer class, you see – but he's in all right, aren't you, Dickie-bird?

DICKINSON. Yes, and glad to be.

PARSONS. So you're in too, Taff – right?

EVANS. Right.

PARSONS (*to* LAWRENCE). That's all of us, chum. So it's settled –

LAWRENCE (*shaking his head, gently*). No.

PARSONS. Why not?

LAWRENCE. It can only mean trouble.

PARSONS (*contemptuously*). Nah. What can they do? Hoof the whole Flight and have the papers talk about a mutiny at Uxbridge? Put us all on jankers and have the story round the whole camp? No. Worst they'll do is collective reprimand. (*In his 'officer' voice'.*) 'None of you understand Service ways, my boys. That's your trouble.' (*Makes a face.*) Best they can do is reconsider –

LAWRENCE. They won't do that…

PARSONS (*obviously agreeing*). Well, it's a chance. There's always a chance, as the bishop said to the housemaid.

LAWRENCE. Don't send it until tomorrow.

PARSONS. Well – we all thought – the sooner the better.

LAWRENCE. No. Not until tomorrow.

PARSONS. All right. Come on, Taff. Well, goodbye, Rossie.

LAWRENCE (*shaking hands*). Goodbye, Sailor.

PARSONS. Come on, Dickie-bird. (*Mutters.*) Err! Officers!
I could bloody well murder them.

He has disappeared. DICKINSON *follows.* EVANS *also
puts his hand out.*

EVANS. Goodbye, Rossie.

LAWRENCE (*shaking hands*). Goodbye, Taff.

EVANS. Good luck for the future.

LAWRENCE. Thank you. The same to you. And thank you for
the – (*Remembering the slang.*) half-dollar.

*EVANS makes a deprecating gesture and is going out as the
FLIGHT-SERGEANT comes in.*

FLIGHT-SERGEANT. What do you think you're doing, young
Evans? Think the break lasts all morning?

EVANS. I was talking to Ross.

FLIGHT-SERGEANT (*roaring*). I don't care if you were
talking to the Aga Khan, get back on fatigue –

EVANS. Yes, Flight. Sorry, Flight.

He flees. The FLIGHT-SERGEANT *comes up to
LAWRENCE.*

FLIGHT-SERGEANT. Ready, boy?

LAWRENCE. Nearly.

He turns to collect some books. The FLIGHT-SERGEANT,
*sitting on the bed, pulls out of the nearly filled kitbag
LAWRENCE's ornamental dagger.*

FLIGHT-SERGEANT. What's this?

LAWRENCE (*carelessly*). Oh – sort of keepsake. Would you
like to have it?

FLIGHT-SERGEANT. Well, thanks. I'll give it to the wife to hang on the wall. She loves stuff like that. I'm telling you, son, you'd have made an airman if the bleeders had only let you be. I told 'em that just now – head bleeder and all.

LAWRENCE. Thank you, Flight. I'm grateful.

FLIGHT-SERGEANT. Didn't work, though. They got it in for you, proper, son – I don't know why. Something to do with your past, shouldn't wonder.

LAWRENCE. Yes. It may be.

FLIGHT-SERGEANT. Well, listen here, my boy, don't let them get you down. What's past is past, see, and finished and dead. What you got to think about is the future. (*Looking at his watch.*) Well – are you ready now?

LAWRENCE (*pulling his kitbag closed and tying it*). Just about.

FLIGHT-SERGEANT. What are you going to do? Any idea?

LAWRENCE (*head bent over kitbag*). Yes. I think I have. I'm going to get back into the RAF as soon as I can.

FLIGHT-SERGEANT (*surprised*). Think you can do that?

LAWRENCE. Well, I'll have to change my name, I suppose. Ross won't do any more. (*Points to the name 'Ross' painted on his kitbag.*) 'Shaw'. I thought of that this morning. How do you like it?

FLIGHT-SERGEANT. All right.

LAWRENCE. But it's not the name that matters. It's the number.

FLIGHT-SERGEANT (*wonderingly*). The number? What number?

LAWRENCE. Oh, any number. Just provided it's one of a lot of others – like this. (*Points to the number on his kitbag.*)

FLIGHT-SERGEANT. I don't know what you're talking about. Do you really want another dose of all this?

LAWRENCE. More than anything else I can think of.

FLIGHT-SERGEANT. You're a glutton for punishment, aren't you?

LAWRENCE (*smiling*). It rather looks like it.

FLIGHT-SERGEANT. I've got to sneak you out through the Group Captain's private entrance. Gawd knows why. I'll get the key. You know his house?

LAWRENCE *nods*.

I'll meet you over there.

He goes out. LAWRENCE *finishes tying his kitbag, shoulders it and turns to exit.*

HAMED'S VOICE (*quiet and clear*). God will give you peace.

LAWRENCE *gives no sign he has heard. He looks round the hut for the last time, then follows the* FLIGHT-SERGEANT *out. A distant bugle call is sounding as –*

The curtain falls.

www.nickhernbooks.co.uk

 facebook.com/nickhernbooks

 twitter.com/nickhernbooks